A NEW KIND OF

CONVERSATION

BLOGGING TOWARD A POSTMODERN FAITH

edited by

Myron Bradley Penner & Hunter Barnes

with contributions by

A NEW KIND OF
CONVERSATION

A New Kind of
CONVERSATION

BLOGGING TOWARD A POSTMODERN FAITH

EDITED BY

MYRON BRADLEY PENNER

AND

HUNTER BARNES

COLORADO SPRINGS · LONDON · HYDERABAD

Authentic Publishing
We welcome your questions and comments.

USA   1820 Jet Stream Drive, Colorado Springs, CO 80921 www.authenticbooks.com
UK   9 Holdom Avenue, Bletchley, Milton Keynes, Bucks, MK1 1QR
      www.authenticmedia.co.uk
India Logos Bhavan, Medchal Road, Jeedimetla Village, Secunderabad 500 055, A.P.

A New Kind of Conversation
ISBN-13: 978-1-932805-58-1
ISBN-10: 1-932805-58-3

Cover design: Paul Lewis
Interior design: Angela Lewis
Editorial team: Andy Sloan, KJ Larson

Printed in the United States of America

Contents

To Abigail, Sophia, and Isabella Penner

AND

To Abigail, Magdalene, and Eden Barnes

ACKNOWLEDGMENTS

It has been a joy for us to put this project together with this group of people. Ellen, Kenzo, Brian, and Bruce: Thank you for your patience, dedication, and great work on this project. This venture also would not have worked without the support and contributions of the many who visited (and continue to visit) the website and posted comments (see below for URL). Thank you to all of you. We further wish to acknowledge Robin Parry of Paternoster, and Volney James of Authentic Media, and express our gratitude to them both for their flexibility and for not only believing in this experiment but also being willing to put their money where their mouths were. Our thanks must go to Leighton Tebay and Prairie Fusion Consulting Inc., as well, for hosting www.anewkindofconversation.com (and contributing to the blog on top of everything else!).

Finally, this book is dedicated to our children: without them the lights in our lives would be dimmer and much, much less joyful. We would like to acknowledge our gratefulness for, and indebtedness to, the grace of our Lord Jesus Christ, which comes to us in so many forms, but principally through our wives, Jodi Penner and Heather Barnes. We love you, and this book could not have happened without your love and support.

PRIMARY BLOGGERS

Bruce Ellis Benson
Professor of Philosophy, Wheaton College

Ellen Haroutunian
writer, speaker, and therapist, Desert Hope Ministries

Mabiala Justin-Robert Kenzo
Professor of Theology, Canadian Theological Seminary

Brian McLaren
pastor, author, speaker, Cedar Ridge Community Church

Myron Bradley Penner
Associate Professor of Philosophy and Theology, Prairie College

At a recent conference I participated with three other philosophers and theologians on a panel that was convened to discuss and debate the significance of postmodern theory for evangelical thought. The procedure for the session was standard practice: each of us would give a brief presentation (20–25 minutes), we would then respond to each other, and afterwards we would field questions from the floor for a few minutes. Since the four of us each had different and in some cases considerably divergent opinions on the subject, and since we all wanted our time in the session to be productive, we agreed to meet together the day before to talk over our perspectives in preparation for the event.

Our conversation that afternoon was more of what you might expect to find at the family dinner table than at an academic conference: free flowing, back and forth, energetic, and stimulating. Areas of appreciation and agreement were discovered and reinforced while other questions were sharpened for further conversation. At the end, we all agreed that our time together had been extremely helpful in clarifying our commonalities as well as our differences and hoped that we would be able to reproduce our conversation in front of an audience the following day.

It was not to be. The context of the event and the format we had agreed upon simply did not allow for the sort of engagement we had enacted the previous day to occur. While our formal session was worthwhile, I couldn't help feeling frustrated by the thought that it could have been much more interesting and illuminating for those present if we had been able to enact something more like the conversational engagement we had shared the previous afternoon.

Books that bring together various individuals for conversation can often fall prey to the same dynamic. In the interest of interaction an author writes a chapter and then responds to the others. A discourse is started but never seems to move beyond the fairly static engagement mandated by the format. To be sure such conference panel discussions and books are helpful and have their place. But having attended and participated in numerous such events at conferences and read my share of such books, I generally find myself wanting something more or different. Something more truly conversational than that which is allowed by the stilted engagements of traditional academic formats.

The present volume achieves this conversational dynamic by following the format of an internet blog. Blogging has become an increasingly popular medium for the exchange and discussion of ideas and anyone who is interested in nearly any topic can go online and get connected to any number of interesting conversations. Here we have in book form an expertly crafted and edited blog on the topic of the relationship of evangelical faith and postmodern theory shaped by some of the leading thinkers writing on the subject today. They are joined by other thoughtful voices that provide the discussion with a truly dialogical quality that makes this book truly unique among introductions to postmodern thought and theology.

Such a format is fitting for an engagement with postmodernity and its interest in fluidity, dynamism, plurality, and open-endedness. It allows the conversation to go on and extend into sometimes unexplored byways and tributaries in all of its multifaceted and never-ending hope and curiosity. Indeed, it may be that in the same way that a revolution in information technology, the advent of the printing press, made the modern world possible as well as giving it its distinctive shape, so another revolution in information technology, the advent of digital technology, will do the same for the postmodern world by allowing the exchange of ideas to take place more conversationally than that which was conceivable within the technological limitations of the early modern world. It will take time before our practices catch up to the new possibilities afforded by digital technology, old ways usually die hard, but as they do they may well look increasingly like the new kind of conversation envisioned and displayed in this book.

In addition to the format, the subject matter is also decisive to the changing conversation concerning Christian faith and practice. As we venture into the twenty-first century the intellectual milieu of Western thought and culture is in a state of transition precipitated by the perceived failure of the philosophical, societal, and ethical assumptions of the modern world spawned by the Enlightenment. This transition has led to an attempt in various fields of inquiry to critique old paradigms and establish new ones to take their place. While this discourse in the aftermath of modernity has produced numerous manifestations of the postmodern condition and divergent opinions and struggles concerning the portrayal of postmodernity in various domains and situations, it has also generated a shared set of common perspectives and defining features that are coalescing into an emergent postmodern paradigm. However, since this new postmodern paradigm is emerging, but neither mature nor regnant, it continues to be hotly contested by those who desire to embrace it for particular purposes as well as those who find reason to oppose it.

As would be expected, the intellectual and cultural transition from modernity to postmodernity is generating serious questions for evangelical Christians. While some have raised concerns about the shifting intellectual and cultural circumstances and suggested that the only appropriate response is to oppose these changes in the interest of maintaining the faith delivered once and for all to the saints, it is important to remember that such challenges are not new for Christian faith, particularly given its missional impulse. The expression of Christianity and Christian teaching has taken shape and been revised and reformed in the context of numerous cultural and historical circumstances. Throughout this history the Christian church has been remarkably adaptable in its task of extending and establishing the message of the gospel in a wide variety of historical and social contexts. If we are to faithfully and appropriately address the opportunities and challenges presented by the postmodern setting without inadvertently accommodating our proclamation of the gospel to the standards of our culture, we must understand the nature of the cultural transition that is occurring as well as its significance for Christian faith and witness.

In this book, leading Christian thinkers enter into genuine and accessible conversation about the opportunities and possibilities of a postmodern Christian faith in a world that is diverse, multifaceted, and constantly in flux. The particular issues they discuss are being engaged and debated by various Christian communities throughout the Anglo-American world as they face the challenge of proclaiming and living out the implications of the Christian faith in the midst of a pluralist and increasingly post-Christian environment. At stake is nothing less than the future of the church and the witness it bears to the liberating news of the gospel of Jesus Christ. I believe that this is the conversation of our time and every time, which is ever new in each particular situation. In both form and content, I know of no better book to introduce readers to this ongoing conversation as it has been made "new" by the advent of the postmodern turn.

JOHN R. FRANKE, DPHIL
PROFESSOR OF THEOLOGY, BIBLICAL SEMINARY

Toward a New Kind of Conversation

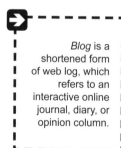

Myron Bradley Penner
and Hunter Barnes

This book is the result of an experiment that started with an online **blog**. But the idea for the entire project, both blog and book, came from a conversation between Robin Parry from Paternoster and Myron about form and content—about how the *form* of many of the discussions of postmodernism is at odds with the *content* of postmodernism. In other words, so many of the books on postmodernism tend to follow a (rather stodgy) traditional academic form, inherited from modern academia, which presents a series of selected essays on various aspects of the topic. What is more, these books tend to be written by those comfortable with Western academia—which means predominantly white, educated males who have been initiated into "the club" (PhD's only, please). This traditional academic form does not breed conversation, but promotes monologue; it does not foster cross-fertilization of ideas, but reinforces one particular perspective on an issue; it is not open to other voices, but is designed precisely to close them off; and, finally, any such discourse is not welcoming to all voices, but privileges a select group who have been properly vetted by the Western academy. All this seems at cross-purposes with any genuinely postmodern discourse.

> *Blog* is a shortened form of web log, which refers to an interactive online journal, diary, or opinion column.

What was needed, Robin and Myron agreed, was a different form for any such book. The idea was to have a genuine dialogue—an exchange of ideas—on the relationship evangelicalism has (or could have) with postmodernism, what a postmodern evangelicalism might look like, etc. However, if this dialogue was to be pursued in a manner that would open up aspects of postmodernism ignored or closed off by current literary forms, certain things would have to be in place. First, we would have to choose our contributors (or "primary bloggers," as we came to call them) carefully. We would need to hear from men and women, Westerners and people from the Two-Thirds World, philosophers and theologians, and practitioners—those involved in evangelical ministry—as well as academics. We began, then, with a list of prospective primary contributors who were both interested in the issue of an evangelical postmodernism and who fit our criteria. We were very pleased when we contacted those on the top of our list and they all said yes: Brian McLaren, a well-known author, speaker, and pastor; Ellen Haroutunian, a Christian therapist who is also heavily involved in church ministry; Mabiala Kenzo, an African theologian and pastor; Bruce Ellis Benson, a Christian philosopher; and Myron Penner, a professor of philosophy and theology. The next question was how to proceed on a project like this, and what sort of forum was needed to facilitate it. Hunter, who was Myron's colleague at the time, supplied the idea of a blog format, which, in addition to fostering the concept of dialogue, also opened up the conversation wider to voices around the world!

The procedure for the book was relatively straightforward. Hunter and Myron began with a list of topics we thought were germane to a conversation on evangelicalism and postmodernism. We then asked each of our primary contributors to write blogs on specific topics, and we posted them, one at a time, on the "A New Kind of Conversation" website (see below for URL). Anyone interested in the topic could interact with the primary blog and the other bloggers who posted responses. After a period of time we pulled the blogs off the Internet and edited them down into a book format. That is what we have here. Our goal in editing has been to present an account of the online conversation in such a way that it is informative and represents the dialogue that actually took place. Having said that, however, the different medium and its constraints, especially in regard to space, mean that this book inevitably transformed features of the online product.

We were forced to select certain **threads** from the comments and leave others out; and we had to excerpt comments, as well as rearrange and edit them for grammar, spelling, and punctuation. We attempted to retain, however, as much of the original spirit of the exchanges as possible and often left in some of the informal expressions typically used in online blogs or text messaging. Brackets in the text ([ ]) indicate an editorial insertion or paraphrase; an ellipsis (. . .) indicates portions we omitted from the text; and the term *sic* indicates that we chose not to change an unconventional spelling or use of grammar. In addition to in-text revisions, we have also inserted explanatory comments into the text so that so that those who are unfamiliar with either the blog-world and its language, or the more technical language used in philosophy and theology, may understand the conversation more easily. The topic of postmodernism and evangelicalism inevitably led the conversation into the heady waters of technical jargon and we felt that rather than edit out difficult terminology, we would keep everyone on the same page by providing working definitions of those terms. Our hope is that our comments and revisions have actually improved the accessibility and usefulness of the product, but readers who are curious about the original, raw version are encouraged to view it online at www.anewkindofconversation.com.

Thread refers to a particular line of conversation on a blog, where various people are commenting and responding to each other on specific topics.

Sic is a Latin word that literally means "so, thus."

One of the biggest challenges we faced, as editors and primary bloggers, in using the "postmodern" medium of the blog was the loss of control. We had very little ability, after writing the primary blog, to determine where the flow of the conversation would go. As editors we also faced challenges insofar as the conversations that naturally developed online did not always easily translate into a preestablished format for our book! All in all we are satisfied with the result, even if a little surprised at certain aspects of it. The project is not without its flaws, we know, but what conversation is perfect? We recognize many things that could improve the project, like participation from North American indigenous peoples, African Americans, and other non-Western peoples. And we could definitely improve the format of the online conversation. But all things considered, we believe this experiment is a good *start* to a new kind of conversation about these issues.

Welcome to the conversation!

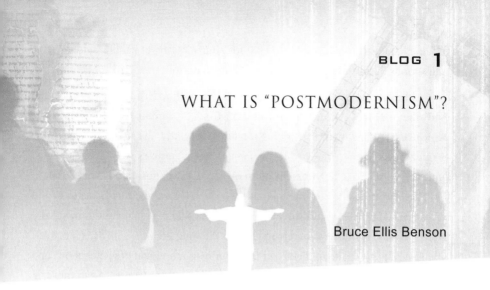

WHAT IS "POSTMODERNISM"?

Bruce Ellis Benson

First, let's get one thing straight: there isn't such a thing as "postmodern-*ism*," i.e., some nicely defined set of beliefs. In fact, the words *postmodern* and *postmodernism* are thrown around so indiscriminately that they often seem to mean just about anything. If you're against "postmodernism," then usually everything bad is "postmodern" (and this often works the other way around). Moreover, the various "postmodernism*s*" in architecture, art, literature, philosophy, social theory, and theology don't exactly mesh (in terms of time periods, characteristics, or theorists). With those crucial caveats in mind, probably the best way of thinking of postmodernism is as an "attitude" (which is how Michel Foucault describes modernity) that is a reaction to the attitude of modernity.

The modern attitude starts with the self. Moderns like René Descartes and Immanuel Kant exhort us to "think for ourselves" (which for Kant is the essence of being "enlightened"). For Descartes, that means setting aside one's beliefs and starting from scratch. For Kant, it means that you rely only on your own reason. Although some moderns, like David Hume, drastically question reason's capacities, generally the modern attitude toward reason was highly positive. It was generally assumed that rational people who had all the facts in hand could come to agreement (at least regarding truths which were "self-evident"). It was likewise assumed that no problems were too big for human reason to handle (though Kant had serious questions about the limits of human reason).

Although critics sometimes charge that the postmodern attitude *also* begins with the self, that attitude is best described as "hypermodernism" (something which one finds, say, in Friedrich Nietzsche). Actually, that point is telling, for it often happens that "modern" philosophers have "postmodern" characteristics, and vice versa. To take Nietzsche as an example, his philosophy is very strongly built around the self, but one couldn't ask for a more vociferous critic of the view that rationality would solve all problems or that it is somehow "universal." Nietzsche is convinced that perceiving and thinking are inherently perspectival, which means we relate to the world from our own individual preconceptions and also those of the culture and communities of which we are a part. As to thinking for ourselves, Foucault shows just how deeply our thinking is mediated by cultural and historical conditions—of which we are often unaware. For Hans-Georg Gadamer, this recognition means that understanding is always communal in the sense that one doesn't simply understand on one's own. Postmodern thinkers argue that the autonomous subject is a human creation—and generally a bad one at that. Emmanuel Levinas has gone so far as to argue that it has made us into egoists and that the only way to change that ethically reprehensible situation is to put the *other* first. With the demise of the autonomous subject has come the demise of the author as supremely powerful. Postmoderns point out that, since no one "owns" language, encapsulating one's meaning in a text is only partially successful. Further, social theorists take the demise of the autonomous subject to mean that much of "who we are" is socially constructed.

Critics of postmodernity often charge that it is just "**relativism**" or "**skepticism**." Certainly the badge of relativism is one that Richard Rorty would gladly wear. But, at least in terms of the major thinkers of postmodernity, that charge generally doesn't fit. Even though it is often leveled against Jacques Derrida, for example, he has gone out of his way to argue that justice is absolute and that meaning is hardly "relative" in the sense of "it can mean whatever you want it to mean." He (rightly) accuses those

> **Relativism** is the view that truth is dependent on the perception of each individual.
>
> **Skepticism** is the view that knowledge is not possible.

who make such accusations of not having read him carefully (or, more likely, not having read him at all). Unfortunately, lack of reading the primary texts of postmoderns is all too typical among critics of postmodernity. Despite all the differences in postmodern thinkers, they would generally agree that 1) we think and know only in connection with others, 2) our knowing is always culturally and historically conditioned, and 3) human reason is considerably less powerful than many **Enlightenment** thinkers assumed. There are, of course, stronger and weaker forms of these theses. Moderns often insist on what they call "realism," the idea that there truly is a "reality out there." Many postmoderns would agree. While there are "antirealists" (such as Rorty) who insist that the world is simply a product of human creation, that is actually the minority view. On the other side, it's hard to imagine anyone flat out denying *any* effect of culture on rea-

> "The Enlightenment" is roughly the same as "Modernity" and refers to the European intellectual movement in the seventeenth and eighteenth centuries which emphasized reason as the key to human knowledge and progress.
>
> *Metaphysics* refers to the theory of reality: what is "really real."
>
> *Epistemology* is the theory of knowledge and deals with questions of what knowledge is and how we know things.

soning. So the question really ends up being how much. Consider the primary example used by a highly acclaimed Christian thinker to argue strenuously in favor of realism: "Lemons are sour." The briefest of examinations of this claim makes it clear that this is a statement as much about human beings as it is about lemons. Yes, *we* find lemons to be sour. But that has to do with our taste buds. So the example actually serves to bolster *both* realism (that there is a world out there in which lemons are sour) *and* the fact that we as human beings happen to find lemons sour. Here it is important to add that there is a huge difference between claiming that there is a "world out there" (a **metaphysical** claim) and claiming that we can know that world "just as it is" (an **epistemological** claim). Postmoderns vary on the extent to which we can know the world "just as it is," but most would not simply give up this distinction. So the charge of "antirealism" against postmodern thinkers is frequently unwarranted.

Given this more humble view of reason in postmodernity, it is hardly surprising that Jean-François Lyotard has defined the term postmodern as "incredulity toward **metanarratives**." Even though Lyotard qualifies this definition by saying he is "simplifying to the extreme," many have (unfortunately) taken this phrase to be the "essence" of postmodernism. What is important about Lyotard's idea of a *grands récits* (literally, "a big story") has to do with both their encompassing nature and their claims to be able to legitimate themselves. To be postmodern is to have "incredulity" toward such stories precisely because they are too encompassing and make claims of legitimation that prove difficult—if not impossible—to substantiate. Note that Lyotard is not talking about "narratives" (which are just stories), but about "metanarratives" (which are stories *about* stories). The metanarrative is designed to legitimate the story.

> *meta* = of a higher or second order; *narrative* = account or story. *Metanarrative* literally refers to the story behind a story, or what explains or makes sense of or justifies an explanation.
>
> *Faith* is used here to refer to something that is believed but not reasoned.
>
> *Linguistic turn* refers to philosophers taking an interest in the role language plays in our thinking and philosophical activity.

So is Christianity such a narrative? There can be no simple answer to that question. Certainly it is a "big story"; yet, since only Christians accept it as true, it is not a "universal" story (even though it is *meant* to be a universal story). Further, to the extent that Christianity is taken to be **"faith,"** then it is a story. But, to the extent that Christianity thinks it can legitimate itself, then it is metanarrative. In other words, we have the premodern and postmodern version of Christianity versus the modern version, in which there is evidence that demands a verdict that can be rendered—so the assumption goes—simply by inspecting the evidence. In contrast, the postmodern conception of Christianity (as the premodern) takes Christianity to be a *faith*, and therefore not subject to the kind of *scientific* legitimation Lyotard has in mind. That does not mean, though, that one has no *reasons* for believing, but postmodern Christians recognize that these reasons cannot pass a test of "universal reason."

A further aspect of most postmodern thought is that our perception of reality is mediated by language (which is often termed the **"linguistic turn"**). Moderns who wish to deny this charge often point to prelinguistic children as examples of thinking without language. Since none of us debating the question of thought being mediated by language are prelinguistic children, that point is simply a nonstarter. My dog (Sir Willoughby) indicates that he's thirsty by going to the kitchen sink and barking at the faucet. It's quite effective and I'm sure it counts as a form of thinking. But that fact doesn't tell us much about *human* thought, nor does the example of prelinguistic children tell us much about linguistic adults. Mediation by language in no way means that there cannot be "direct" experience. I can still "directly" perceive something. Yet, since that perception itself is always affected by categories of thought and thus language, then there is still mediation. But those who object to postmodernism often argue that if thinking is mediated by language and language is itself always cultural and historical in nature, then thinking ends up being purely **contingent**. That, of course, is Rorty's view. Yet that is hardly the obvious conclusion. While categories of thought/language vary from culture to culture (not to mention within cultures), that variance is neither absolute nor unbridgeable. To take an ethical example, most cultures have a basic ethos that calls for honoring one's parents. But *how* one honors them varies not only from culture to culture but also from family to family within any given culture. So here we have what seems to be a universal that is instantiated in various ways. To see *only* the universal or *only* the particular is to miss what is a complex phenomenon. My own formula for that phenomenon is this: "In our similarities, there are

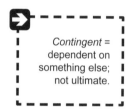

Contingent = dependent on something else; not ultimate.

differences; in our differences, there are similarities." That linguistically mediated concepts are not *exactly the same* from culture to culture nor from person to person does not spell the end of reason, morality, or truth (though it does make things more complicated than moderns thought them to be).

Finally, along with the linguistic turn goes a turn to narrative. Simply put, postmoderns tend to think of human existence as being part of a story. Stories are the ways we define and understand ourselves, as well as others. So we have political stories, religious stories, personal stories, family stories, community stories—and that's merely a sampling. Critics of postmoderns often latch on to the word *story* (or *narrative*) and assume that story = fiction. Yet stories can be true or false. Moreover, despite many ideas to the contrary, the postmodern choice is *not* one between "propositions" and "narratives." The two are perfectly compatible. Stories always contains propositions (such as "Jesus rose from the dead") and propositions presume the stories in which they are set (so truth claims about the efficacy of a medical technique presume the whole story of what we call "modern medicine"). The main difference between moderns and postmoderns is generally whether they take propositions or stories to be primary. Postmodern Christians see Christianity as a narrative around which they orient their lives.

COMMENTS

THREAD ONE:
POSTMODERNISM AND CHRISTIANITY

- Greg McRitchie: **How can postmodern philosophy be used by Christians?**

It is with some trepidation that I offer what appears to be the first comment, but here goes. I am struck by the overabundant use of philosophy that at its core is antithetical to Christianity to attempt to establish a "new" kind of foundation for Christianity. If the philosophers you quoted were all either **agnostic** or in some cases virulently **atheistic**, what makes you think you can start with their presuppositions and produce a different result?

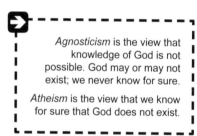

Agnosticism is the view that knowledge of God is not possible. God may or may not exist; we never know for sure.

Atheism is the view that we know for sure that God does not exist.

- Bruce Ellis Benson: **On using secular philosophy**

Greg (kudos to you for having the courage to be the first respondent): You wonder whether using the presuppositions of agnostics or atheists is appropriate. Well, my first response is that we certainly need to be careful about adopting presuppositions that are at odds with the Christian faith. Having said that, adopting/adapting from non-Christian/pagan/atheistic philosophers is something that Christians have been doing since the early days of Christianity. Take the first chapter of John's Gospel: in naming Jesus the *logos*, John is tapping a deep Greek philosophical mine. The **pre-Socratic philosopher** Heraclitus had said that the *logos* orders the cosmos. In saying that Jesus was that *logos*, John was using Greek philosophy to make a heavy-duty **metaphysical** statement about just who Jesus is. Despite **Tertullian's** famous (rhetorical) question—"What has Athens to do with Jerusalem?"—many of the early church fathers used ideas from Greek philosophy in their theology. Indeed, some contemporary theologians protest that they did so inappropriately! The **open theists**, for instance, complain that Christian ideas about God have long been far too shaped by pagan philosophy. In any case, it was **Augustine** who talked of "plundering the Egyptians," by which he meant drawing on the resources of philosophy. In his case, it was the pagan philosopher Plato. In **Thomas Aquinas'** case, it was the pagan philosopher Aristotle. Contemporary evangelical philosophers often draw on the atheist **Bertrand Russell** (who wrote a famous essay titled "Why I Am Not a Christian") for his theory of the correspondence theory of truth. That Russell thought the statement "God exists" does not correspond to any existing state of affairs in no way means that his theory of truth can't be used by Christians. Similarly, while one has to be vigilant when working with agnostic or atheistic philosophy, there is no reason to think that a Foucault or a Derrida has nothing to teach us.

> In ancient Greek, *logos* literally means "word," but also refers to "reason" or "explanation."
>
> The term *pre-Socratic philosophy* refers to philosophy before Socrates, who lived c. 470–399 BC.
>
> Recall that the term *metaphysics* refers to what is really real.
>
> Tertullian (c. 155–235 AD) was a second-century Christian theologian.
>
> *Open theism* refers to a small, but influential and growing, group of evangelicals who reject the idea in traditional theology that God does not change. They also reject the idea that God knows the future, on the basis that the future, by definition, is not knowable
>
> Augustine (354–430) was the bishop of Hippo (in North Africa) and one of the early church's greatest philosophers and theologians.
>
> Thomas Aquinas (usually just called Thomas) lived in the thirteenth century and was one of the greatest Christian thinkers of the Middle Ages, or any other age.
>
> Bertrand Russell was a well-known philosophical atheist from the early twentieth century. He taught philosophy at Cambridge University.

- Leighton Tebay: **Why is there postmodernism?**

I think a better question might be "Why is there postmodernism?" I see Bruce Benson's point in saying there's no such thing as postmodernism, but there is something very real happening in Western society today. That is why a number of missionaries and church planters have reexamined the structure of the church, the focus of our mission, and even the authenticity of our message. The sad reality is that whatever age we are in seems to have a caustic effect on evangelical churches. Those who are more likely to be labeled "postmodern" are less likely to be evangelical. The big question for many of us is why.

As a member of a generation that is often labeled "postmodern," I'd say my "Incredulity toward metanarratives" comes from two main things:

. . . The *first* one is easy to understand. If I were try to buy a car and I consulted salespeople from Chevrolet, Pontiac, Buick, Ford, Lincoln, Toyota, Honda, Acura, BMW, and Volkswagen and each of them told me they had the best car for me, which one would I believe? I am most likely to view all the data from my biased perspective. I'm a Chev man, with a grudging respect for Toyotas and Hondas. The Ford guy might have offered me the best deal possible on a Taurus, but because I'm a Chev guy and I'd have to eat way too many words if I drove a Ford I would convince myself some other car is the better deal. I am also likely to have an inherent distrust of anyone telling me something in order to make money. I know the salesperson is highly motivated to get me to make a decision and strongly biased. Ultimately I wouldn't know whom to believe. I think this illustrates why "postmodernism" exists. We have hundreds, if not thousands, of competing ideologies, approaches, and philosophies in an increasingly **pluralistic** culture and people don't know what to believe. Logically, either one

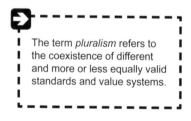

The term *pluralism* refers to the coexistence of different and more or less equally valid standards and value systems.

of these voices is right or none of them are right. Some are more right than others. In response to this, people begin to pick and choose what they want from each stream of thought and cobble together their own worldview.

The *second* factor stems from a distrust of accepted sources of authority and truth. If politicians lie, and the media misrepresent, and [my parents,] who were supposed to raise me, abandoned me, it [would begin] to wear down one's confidence in any voice claiming to hold an exclusive claim to the truth. When a significant portion of a generation loses a parent in childhood, it has a dramatic effect on how society views authority and truth. Even though kids may not be able to articulate it, deep down they know they were wronged. If they are wronged by those who ought to have been the most faithful to them, they are naturally disinclined to trust others in the same way.

- Greg McRitchie: **"Postmodern Christian" or "Post-Christian modernist"?**

Leighton: All cars (Lada excepted) get you from A to B. Therefore one choice is as good as the next. Not so with truth. The "attitude" of postmodernism undermines even the concept of truth in favor of a relativistic view of every man for himself. Even if you expand this to every group for themselves and then expand the definition of the group to all humanity, if you accept the criticism of Kant then we are still hopelessly cut off from a transcendent view of truth as it corresponds to God in his essence, nature, and character. I like how R. C. Sproul once put it, "Kant says we can't, but Paul (Romans 1:18 [and through verse 20]) says we can" (my paraphrase). It does us no good if "the real world" is out there but we can't know it. [Francis] Schaeffer acknowledged this problem in *He Is There and He Is Not Silent*,[1] but noted that all that is necessary is that we have sufficient knowledge as opposed to exhaustive. It seems to me that postmodern Christians are throwing up their hands and declaring that knowledge must be exhaustive or it's no use at all. That being the case, it is more likely we will be producing post-Christian modernists, rather than any kind of meaningfully Christian disciples.

- Marc Vandersluys: **Postmodern Christians and mystery**

Greg: All cars *might* get you from A to B; you won't have that certainty until you've actually driven those cars between the two points (and you'll never be certain about the following trip either, until you make it). Furthermore, Car 1 might get you to point B faster; Car 2, while slower, will get better fuel economy.

Car 3 is cheaper than Car 4, but is more likely to break down halfway to point B. My point is simply that there are more factors than A to B to consider.

I wonder if you aren't mixing up the two "isms" in question here. Schaeffer, according to what you have stated, would actually hold a somewhat postmodern view. As I understand it, and as this essay posits, moderns insisted that we *can* have exhaustive (or, at least, absolute) knowledge. Rather than insisting on exhaustive knowledge or nothing at all (a rather modern thing to do), postmoderns suggest that exhaustive knowledge *is not humanly possible* and that this is OK. "Postmodern Christians," then, would assert the same thing, saying it is OK to not know, to doubt. We fill the gaps with faith, embracing some level of mystery.

- Greg McRitchie: **Postmodern leaps of faith and relativism**

Thanks for your interesting comments, Marc. . . . Thinking about what you said prompted me to reread parts of Schaeffer last night. You are certainly right, in that he definitely was not a modernist, but that does not mean he was postmodern either. In fact he argued equally against both extremes. He never rejected reason, because one would have to use reason to deny reason; and that would obviously be self-refuting. What he did reject (and rightly so) was the **rationalism** that was a natural consequence of the Enlightenment's skeptical conclusion of philosophical **naturalism**. Man (notes Schaeffer), starting only from himself and using *only* reason, always ends in despair. If there is nothing transcendent outside of ourselves, then there are no universals to give meaning to our particulars. Schaeffer blames this on Aquinas. Sproul

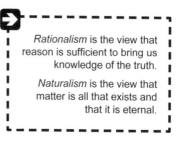

Rationalism is the view that reason is sufficient to bring us knowledge of the truth.

Naturalism is the view that matter is all that exists and that it is eternal.

swears he should lay it at the feet of Kant, but agrees with his analysis. Kant seemed to realize what he had done, and proposed a postmodern "leap of faith" divorced from reason, because the world seems to work better if we pretend there is a God.

Schaeffer is equally critical of this "upper story leap," as he called it, because it is divorced from reason. The result guts the Christian gospel and reduces it to nothing but a relativistic story that can be ignored or can be embraced without consequence, because it's not "really" true. As long as people are willing to compartmentalize their faith and not make any dogmatic assertions that actually make claims on how people live their lives, then modernism is happy to leave us alone. It is an error to reject the proper use of reason because of the excess of rationalism. It is even more egregious to make an **existential leap** into **mysticism** and call that "authentic" Christianity. That is actually the response of those who have acquiesced to modernism's analysis and looks very similar to what others call "postmodernism."

> The term *existential* refers to existence, and the act or process of existing in particular. An existential leap refers to a passionate, subjective acceptance of something that we find objectively meaningless or absurd.
>
> *Mysticism* in this context refers to a noncognitive, affective, and intuitive encounter with God, as opposed to a rational understanding of God.

Now I know Dr. Benson has tried to deflect the fact that "critics of postmodernity often charge that it is just 'relativism' or 'skepticism.'" However, in simply stating that "Jacques Derrida . . . has gone out of his way to argue that justice is absolute and that meaning is hardly 'relative' in the sense of 'it can mean whatever you want it to mean,'" Benson has (so far) failed to assuage my initial concern that it is even possible to start with the radical epistemological skepticism of these "postmodern thinkers" and end up with anything resembling biblical Christianity.

Perhaps I am wrong, but he will have to do more work to convince me. Like a math teacher, I don't just want the answer—I want him to show me how he got it. So for now I'm giving him half marks.

• Leighton Tebay: **Paul and modern approaches to knowledge**

Greg: I agree with you that there are good choices and bad choices. My point is that in our pluralistic society it isn't easy to pick out the best choice. Within the Christian faith there are dozens of distinct major streams, and you can find people in each one that are convinced they are more right than the rest. How does the average person sort this through?

Paul was sure of what he believed. So sure that he cast his old life to the side and embraced a journey that led him into suffering, scorn, and rejection by his own people. His example is a challenge to those who subscribe to the belief that we can't be sure of anything. How did Paul come to that confidence? I don't think it was by reasoning through the competing philosophies of his day. The modern road doesn't end with the kind of confidence that Paul had. It leads to arrogance and knowledge that "puffs up." In the next era of the church we will need to find a deeper, purer, perhaps more selfless kind of confidence that inspires faith.

- Bruce Benson's response: **St. Paul vs. modern approaches to knowledge**

To Leighton Tebay: "Why is there postmodernism?" is certainly a good question (though it wasn't the question that the blog organizers asked me to write about). You're right that there are various competing narratives, though they're not all equally true. Moreover, you're right that sorting them out isn't simple or easy. And that's true even regarding competing theologies within Christianity (say,

Calvinism and **Arminianism**). One of the consequences of the end of modernity is that the supposed consensus of modernity (and I say "supposed" because modern thought is much more diverse than we usually think) no longer exists. On the one hand, that's scary to many people, because the confidence that we all reasoned alike was reassuring. On the other hand, modernity had a very particular conception of reason, one that was generally hostile to "faith."

Theology based on the teachings of John Calvin, which emphasizes God's sovereignty and grace.

Theology based on the teachings of Jacob Arminius (and often in opposition to Calvinists), which emphasizes human freedom and responsibility.

While we're on the subject of "faith," your comment regarding Paul is appropriate. Paul makes it clear in 1 Corinthians that knowledge claims often "puff up" (1 Corinthians 8:1). I take it that he means claims that are arrogant in the sense that they claim more knowledge than they truly have. But I also take it that this arrogance springs from thinking that our knowledge stems from us. Paul says that anyone who claims to know something does not yet have the necessary knowledge (v. 2). But then he [immediately] goes on to give a kind of reversal: "[anyone] who loves God is known by God" (v. 3) We find this same strange sort of reversal in Galatians 4:9, where Paul begins by saying, "But now that you know God," but then he quickly corrects himself by adding, "or rather are known by God." It seems to me that the implication is that our knowledge is a gift to us, that our knowledge of God is preceded by our being known by God. Paul also makes it clear—in that oft-quoted passage—that our knowledge is partial and incomplete (1 Corinthians 13:12). That's just part of what it means to be finite (which is how God made us to be). This in no way precludes truth or knowledge claims, but it does mean that we do not know as God knows. Call that "postmodern," if you like. Or just call it biblical. The Bible has always been at odds with the pretensions of human knowledge put forth in modernity (or the Enlightenment).

- Myron Bradley Penner: **Postmodernism, reason, and authority**

One brief comment. As I shall say in one of my later blogs for this project, one of my favorite ways to narrate the shifts from premodernity to modernity to postmodernity is around the changing attitudes toward and conceptions of the sources and forms of authority (for belief and practice). This approach places the modern-postmodern shift in a particular theological light—one that Bruce Benson has developed at book-length in his *Graven Ideologies: Nietzsche, Derrida & Marion on Modern Idolatry* (InterVarsity, 2002). (Highly recommended, **BTW**.) I think most of us "evangelicals" who are convinced that we must get over modernity are so convinced because we are troubled by the modern **apotheosis** of human reason (roughly defined as "universal and objective"). The twentieth-century evangelical **apologetic** effort seems motivated primarily by making the same move as modern theological liberals, only as its obverse. That is, liberal theologians reacted to the modern emphasis on reason as authoritative with a hearty "Amen!" and then proceeded to demythologize, higher criticize, and

> BTW = "by the way"
>
> *Apotheosis* occurs when we take something from the created order and attribute divine status to it—like the ancient Pharaohs or Roman Caesars.
>
> *Apologetics* is the rational defense of the faith.

otherwise revise the faith in light of rational critiques of Christianity. Evangelical apologists (Francis Schaeffer included), on the other hand, said something like, "You might be right that human reason is authoritative, but you're completely wrong that orthodox biblical faith is thereby falsified—and let us prove that to you using only reasons that are universal and objective!" And so ensued a century of rational apologetic efforts. Postmodernism, especially as described here by Bruce, is *not* opposed to rational discourse, nor even the rational articulation of Christian belief; rather it is opposed to a particular conception of reason and the idea that this flawed conception of reason is the final arbiter for Christian belief and practice.

• Bruce Ellis Benson: **A(n impossible) conversation on The Impossible**

First, thanks for all of your thoughtful and respectful postings. This promises to be a real conversation, not just people talking at one another.

Having only a thousand words to write on the phenomenon dubbed "postmodernism" was a tall order. I'm sure I've been, at best, only partially successful (if that). So, for example, it was impossible to lay out the case that Jacques Derrida isn't a relativist as part of those 1,000 words. To Greg McRitchie, then, you might want to look at some of the other things I've written on Derrida in which I lay out that case (*Graven Ideologies* is one of those texts—BTW, Myron, thanks for the kind words about that text). Of course, don't take my word for it! Read, say, Derrida's "Afterword" in *Limited Inc²* (in which Derrida explicitly denies being a relativist) or "The Mystical Foundation of Authority" in *Acts of Religion³* (in which he says that justice is not **deconstructible**).

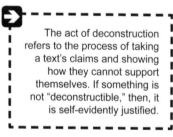

The act of deconstruction refers to the process of taking a text's claims and showing how they cannot support themselves. If something is not "deconstructible," then, it is self-evidently justified.

THREAD TWO:
RORTY AND LYOTARD

• Bob Robinson: **Lyotard and Augustinian Christianity**

When you think about it, Lyotard is almost *Augustinian* in his demand that faith always precedes reason—that we believe in order to understand. According to Lyotard, the problem with universal narratives is not that they are "big stories" but that they seek to prove they are valid by way of reason as the ultimate arbitrator. As I understand Lyotard, he is arguing that the Enlightenment belief in Reason [*sic*] is as much faith as is any other religion, only it denies it the whole time, deceiving everyone that buys into it.

This, I submit, is not antithetical to Christian faith; rather, it is antithetical to modern philosophy (with its grounding in "Reason" as the basis for all knowledge, as if "Reason" existed outside the parameters of any person's belief system).

What many Christians are reacting against in postmodernity is not Lyotard's definition of postmodernity, but a *Neo-Lyotardism* that takes this rather complex understanding of "metanarrative" and simplifies it to just meaning "we must be suspicious of all grand stories." This neo-Lyotardism is indeed a challenge to the grand story presented in the Bible, for it has crept into the public consciousness and is expressed by some "postmodern critics" of Christianity.

There are a number of possible Christian responses to neo-Lyotardism, but the first response is this: *Let's get Lyotard right!* Christians can point out that his definition of postmodernism is not against the grand story just because it is big and seeks to explain all of life; rather, Lyotard said that postmodernity, ultimately, is skeptical when anybody presents a grand story and then says it is true because Reason proves it to be so. He actually is saying that all of life is explained by narrative and myth, that the only way to understand reality is through story and faith in those stories.

- Bruce Ellis Benson: **Repudiating narratives is impossible**

To Bob Robinson: You call for getting Lyotard "right," and I think you've done it! When you write that "postmodernity, ultimately, is skeptical when anybody presents a grand story and then says it is true because Reason proves it to be so," you've accurately described what Lyotard is saying. The repudiation of narratives, of course, is simply impossible: even the repudiation of a narrative would prove to be another narrative. So the question is not whether we should have them, but rather what kind of justification we think we can give them.

- Marius Mazuru: **Richard Rorty a relativist?**

I find myself agreeing with most of Bruce's analysis of postmodernity. Just one disagreement: I believe he misread or misinterpreted **Rorty**. In a number of books, particularly in *Objectivity, Relativism, and Truth*,[1] Rorty goes to great lengths to explain that (and why) he is *not* a relativist—that would be a self-refuting position. He would definitely not accept the idea that "the world is simply a product of human creation" either, unless by the world we mean culture and civilization. And, he *is* one of the major thinkers of postmodernity; his views are definitely not fringe, minority views.

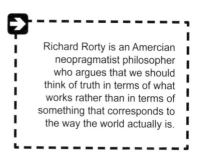

Richard Rorty is an Amercian neopragmatist philosopher who argues that we should think of truth in terms of what works rather than in terms of something that corresponds to the way the world actually is.

Since I write my comment after both Bruce Benson and Brian McLaren posted their articles, I find it interesting to note the difference between the approach to postmodernity of someone from a background in philosophy [like Benson] as opposed to [the approach to postmodernity of] someone with a literary background [like McLaren]. We need all the different perspectives to keep ourselves sane and balanced. I look forward to the conversation!

- Bruce Ellis Benson: **Rorty as a kind of relativist**

To Marius Mazuru: You're right that Richard Rorty in an important sense doesn't want to be a relativist. In fact, he wants to shift the way we talk so that we simply give up the term "relativism," because its opposite—"absolutism"—doesn't exist (see the introduction to Rorty's book, *Philosophy and Social Hope*[2]). But, as an ironist who freely admits that his positions cannot be grounded by rational argumentation, he recognizes that he is a relativist of a certain sort. In "Solidarity or Objectivity?" (in *Objectivity, Relativism, and Truth*[3]), he distinguishes between three types of relativism. While he rejects the first two (the first as self-refuting and the second as "eccentric"), he claims to hold the third, viz., "that there is nothing to be said about either truth or rationality apart from our descriptions of the familiar procedures of justification which a given society—ours—uses" (p. 23). Of course, then he goes on to wonder whether "relativist" is the right term for this description. Perhaps it's not—and that might be an ongoing conversation. But, as it turns out, most people would call this position "relativist" (a point that he recognizes).

Perhaps the phrase "the world is simply a product of human creation" over-simplifies Rorty's view (which I certainly don't want to do). Yet, when he says that the pragmatist "does not think that his views correspond to the nature of things" (ibid.), that seems reasonably close to the idea of the "world" being a cul-turally conditioned, human creation. But, again, perhaps that formulation is still too simple. I do want to do justice to Rorty's views. One last thing: at least in the world of philosophy, Rorty's ideas are considered fringe views. Yet, as you note, my article was definitely written from a philosophical view, and I well recognize that. But I'm with you when you say "we need all the different perspectives to keep ourselves sane and balanced." So thanks for your helpful comments.

THREAD THREE:
METANARRATIVES, IDEOLOGY, AND OPPRESSION

Ideology refers to a system of beliefs or set of values that is unquestioningly adopted by a group of people or society and is used to influence or coerce agreement.

• Brian McLaren: **Hitler, Stalin, and the dangers of metanarratives**

A few years ago, I engaged in an online dialogue with a well-known evangelical who had declared "Postmodernism is dead" in light of September 11, 2001. He had defined postmodernism, just as Bruce Benson says we shouldn't, and I was trying (less effectively than Bruce has done) to correct his misconception. In so doing, I tried to offer a bit of social history to augment the intellectual history. I've paraphrased here what I wrote in my reply a couple years ago, not to contradict what Bruce has written (because I fully agree with him), but to supplement it.

In the late twentieth century, many thoughtful people of a postmodern attitude looked back at regimes like Stalin's and Hitler's. (One must never forget how the postmodern attitude developed in the aftermath of the Holocaust and colonialism, as deeply ethical European intellectuals like **Michael Polanyi** reflected on the atrocities their peers had perpetuated or acquiesced to.) They realized that these **megalomaniacs** used grand systems of belief to justify their atrocities. Those **totalitarian** systems of belief—which these people sometimes called "metanarratives," but which also could have been called "worldviews" or "ideologies"— were so powerful that they could transform good European intellectuals into killers or accomplices. These thoughtful intellectuals thought back over European history and real-

Michael Polanyi (1891–1976) was an influential scientist and philosopher of science who argued against the notion that science or any other knowledge is purely objective, and instead argued that all knowledge includes and depends upon a personal, tacit dimension.

A *megalomaniac* is someone with delusions of grandeur or an obsessive belief in their own omnipotence.

Totalitarianism here refers to a system of belief or ideology that forcibly regulates every facet of life, both social and private; usually this coincides with a "police state" in which beliefs are monitored and enforced by military power.

ized (as C. S. Lewis did) that those who have passionate commitment to a system of belief will be most willing not only to die for it, but to kill for it as well.

These same thoughtful postmodern people looked at the powerful belief systems of the twentieth-century worldviews (extreme Marxism is one such worldview), grand stories (anti-Semitism is one such story, white supremacy is another, American manifest destiny is another), and ideologies (such as the industrialist ideology that the earth and its resources are not God's creation deserving care through reverential stewardship, but rather are simply natural resources there for the taking by secular industrialists), and they were horrified. Again and again these dominating belief systems were responsible for so many millions of deaths, so much torture, so much loss of freedom and dignity, so much damage to the planet. As a result, large numbers of thoughtful and ethically sensitive people sought to undermine the dominance of potentially destructive belief systems by advocating incredulity or skepticism toward them. Perhaps this was an overreaction, but then again, wasn't some sort of skeptical reaction needed?

In more recent history, the "metanarrative" of the **Taliban** and other radical Islamists simply adds another reason for incredulity or skepticism toward belief systems which seek control by force or intimidation. And rightly or wrongly, the US action in Iraq may convince many people around the world that we're just another powerful elite bent on domination, coercion, and elimination of our opponents through a **messianic** metanarrative of American empire.

> The *Taliban* (literally = "seeker of knowledge") are Sunni Islamic fundamentalists dedicated to instituting strict, conservative Islamic law in Afghanistan, Iraq and other Middle Eastern countries, through military and guerilla warfare if necessary.
>
> *Messianic* here refers to the belief that someday one's system of beliefs or social structure will be vindicated as the truth and unbelievers will be forced to acknowledge and accept it.

Incredulity toward metanarratives, then, can be understood as common sense: After you've seen millions of people killed by other people who felt they had a right, based on their metanarrative, to do so, not to maintain some degree of incredulity would be stupid—wouldn't it?

Meanwhile, that incredulity created problems of its own, not the least of which is this: If one doubts all systems of belief, all ideologies, all universal stories, what does one live by—self-interest? If big stories are dangerous to live by, are small stories better, or no stories? Is that possible? Won't the absence of big stories and big ideas and comprehensive belief systems leave people vulnerable to relativism and narcissism and consumerism?

So, some people are worried that "postmoderns" will embrace relativism as an excuse to do anything they want. But other people are still worried that "moderns" will use their absolutism as an excuse to do anything they want—and the "moderns" tend to have more and bigger weapons. One side is against the other's supposed denial of truth in the interest of self-indulgence, and the other side is against its opposite's apparent monopolization of truth in the interest of political or religious domination. Many of us are convinced that both sides are right about each other's danger. We are seeking a way to be faithful Christians while taking both dangers seriously. We may not have all the details worked out yet. But these things take time.

- Bruce Ellis Benson: **Both sides are dangerous!**

I couldn't agree more with Brian's comments. His historical contextualization is crucial to understanding why postmoderns would be leery of grand stories. So many atrocities have been committed in their name (and, sadly, even in the name of the narrative of Christianity). The "solution" to the dangers of grand stories (as if there were such a neat, simple thing as a "solution") is not the renunciation of them in the name of relativism. Like Brian, I am "convinced that both sides are right about each other's danger" and that taking both dangers seriously is part of what it means to be faithful Christians.

- Greg McRitchie: **Logic is an essential property of God**

I have to say that after reading Brian's comments several times and thinking seriously about them, I find myself getting more dismayed every time I read them. First, not only are they logically **fallacious**, but it is insulting to thinking Christians to compare them (even if it is only implied,

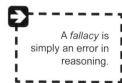

A *fallacy* is simply an error in reasoning.

which it clearly is) to Stalin, Hitler, and the Taliban simply because they hold to a biblical view of truth. Let's see: Hitler brushed his teeth so all people who brush their teeth are suspect. . . . The problem with Hitler and Stalin was not that they thought they were [ideologically] *right*; the problem with them is that they were *wrong* and *evil*. Even the supposed postmodern reaction presupposes the thought that they were wrong and evil.

Do you, Brian, think that you are right that they were wrong? The whole notion that underlies postmodernism is **self-referentially incoherent**, and no amount of tinkering with words is going to change that. *Logic is an essential property of God*. The laws of logic are essential, unavoidable, principles of human thought and being. We cannot not use them, because we are made in the image of God.

> *Self-referentially incoherent* means that an idea or position contradicts itself.
>
> An *essential property* is an attribute of a thing that can't be taken away from it without changing what it is—that is, it is what makes the thing what it is. Greg is saying here that logic is part of what makes God who he is.

Maybe I am just not spiritual enough to see it, but the postmodern Emperor does not appear to be wearing any clothes.

• Myron Bradley Penner: **Truth, logic, and sin**

To Greg McRitchie: I appreciate your bringing up some of these important questions and am glad you feel free to enter into conversation about them. I want to fashion a brief response to your comments on Brian's Hitler-Stalin analogy.

I understand the point of Brian's analogy differently than you. The way I read him, the gist of Brian's analogy is *not* to say that because Hitler and Stalin believed they were right Christians should deny they have the truth; nor is Brian saying that Christians who say they have the truth are genocidal maniacs. Rather (and Brian may correct me if I am wrong), Brian's mention of Hitler and Stalin concerns the source of their confidence for the "truths" they believe. Hitler and Stalin have confidence they are right because they make the modern assumption that the guiding lights of natural reason are sufficient to give them access to what is really real, truly true, etc.

Perhaps, as you say, logic is an essential attribute of God's nature, and reason is required to establish all beliefs as true in advance of faith. I, however, am more inclined toward the Augustinian view espoused above by Jon Wood [in an earlier post Jon had appealed to St. Augustine to make the point that faith comes before understanding], and one looks in vain for direct biblical warrant for the claim that logic is part of God's essential nature. But let's just say you're right about God's logical nature—after all, we cannot do without logic, so perhaps God cannot either. The problem with your appeal to logic to sort things out is that logic only has relevance when used by humans in the context of everyday life. And the trouble with humans is that we are notably fallible, finite, and sinful. As I learned in my freshman logic class, logical fallacies are **incorrigible**, so that even though we study them and know

In this context, *incorrigible* means that we cannot help but commit errors when we reason.

Formal validity is a logical term that refers to the correct structure of an argument (the way it is organized) as opposed to the truth of its content (what it actually says).

Euclidean geometry (discovered and developed by the Greek mathematician Euclid in the fourth century BC) is geometry done on a two-dimensional surface. Euclidean geometry is able to provide conclusive proof of its theorems, as there was only one frame of reference. Non-Euclidean geometry is geometry done on a three-dimensional plane, which posits a potentially infinite number of consistent geometric frameworks.

Bivalent logic is a logic that is structured around only two possible truth values for any statement, true or false.

all about them, we still make them all the time. What is more, the truth values of our conclusions are only indirectly related to the **formal validity** of our arguments. This means that:

1. We may have our logic straight as far as is humanly demonstrable and still not have finally got it right as God sees it (earlier Jon mentioned the failure of set theory in mathematics, but we should also add that the proliferation of **non-Euclidean geometries** militates against the absoluteness of **bivalent logics**); and

2. In the application of our logical arguments—however logically consistent and true (formally) they may be—we may use them to do evil rather than good.

The problem with Hitler and Stalin, as you rightly note, is that they were evil and immoral, not that they were irrational and illogical—though perhaps they were crazy. (I am reminded here of Søren Kierkegaard's "objective lunatic," in Johannes Climacus' *Concluding Unscientific Postscript to Philosophical Fragments*, who escapes from the asylum and devises a plan to avoid detection by focusing on an objective truth. He ties a small ball to his coattails, and every time it hits him in the rump he loudly proclaims, "The world is round!" Of course, far from convincing people of his sanity, this declaration of an objective, logical truth is evidence of his lunacy!) I guess that Brian (and I) are worried that Christians tend to compare the evil in the hearts of Stalin and Hitler with their own sinful proclivities and judge their "Christian sins" as morally and qualitatively *better* forms of sin.

To sum up, the example of Hitler and Stalin offers us an illustration of just how wrong human reason can be, left to its own devices. We could point to the Crusades as an example of Christian abuses of power and reason, but also recent evangelicalism can boast of its own list of dictatorial leaders—some famous, but many more obscure—who have abused and damaged people's lives, all in the name of their presumed access to the absolute truth through Scripture. I think the lesson to be learned from the Hitler-Stalin analogy is that the confident proclamation of Christian truth does not rest upon the ability of human reason to access absolute foundations for knowledge and truth, but rather upon God's grace and mercy to us in Jesus Christ. We surely will continue to proclaim the truth of the gospel, but with an added sensitivity to our own tendencies to distort the gospel of Jesus Christ.

- Brian McLaren: **Stalin and Hitler**

Please be assured: I wasn't comparing thinking Christians—or unthinking ones—to Stalin and Hitler. I'm sorry that my posting came across that way to at least one reader. No insult was intended. I was simply trying to offer an explanation for one of the significant social concerns that gave rise to the famous phrase "incredulity to metanarratives."

All of us—myself included—are probably more aware of the dangers of other people's metanarratives than our own. For that reason, I would hope Christians—

who have been instructed by Jesus to concentrate on the obstructions in our own eyes before we attempt eye surgery on our neighbor—would be among the first to engage in self-examination regarding the ways we have allowed ourselves to slip into inexcusable behavior (anti-Semitism, racism, witch-burning, etc.) through history. And I hope we would be among the last to become defensive, as if none of those inexcusable behaviors exist, or as if acknowledging them would make us worse Christians. Personally, I trust people more who admit they've made mistakes. And I think the Christian community will become more trustworthy when we make a full acknowledgement of our mistakes through history. Perhaps we need our own "**truth and reconciliation commission**." Stalin and Hitler seem to have been governed by minds incapable of much in the way of moral regret or self-examination. Sadly, an aversion to regret and self-examination is common—as Myron wisely suggests—to all sinful creatures like ourselves. Our status as Christians—thinking or otherwise—doesn't seem immediately to cure us of this aversion.

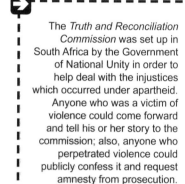

The *Truth and Reconciliation Commission* was set up in South Africa by the Government of National Unity in order to help deal with the injustices which occurred under apartheid. Anyone who was a victim of violence could come forward and tell his or her story to the commission; also, anyone who perpetrated violence could publicly confess it and request amnesty from prosecution.

THREAD FOUR:
Miscellaneous Comments on
Defining Christian Postmodernism

• Eric Mason: **New openness and freedom in postmodernity**

So much of the fun of this new conversation about Christianity and philosophy is an openness to regard all ways of knowing Christ, in the history of knowing Christ, as possibilities again. Orthodoxy has become simple again, at least as simple as the orthodoxy of Christ can be. There is a freedom in the insecurity of postmodernism. I don't know anything more than you do and what we can know is limited anyway. But what we can know is, as the article said, our narrative. There is in this a mighty and final reformation of the people as grand as the first German Bible for Germans. As dangerous as allowing the average man or woman to interpret the Scriptures is the danger of subjective truth under the guidance of the Word and the Holy Spirit. The fires of revolution burn in these postmodern words, "Who is Christ to you?" Our challenge is the generosity of listening and the philanthropy of the open forum. But the rewards are a deeper knowledge of an infinitely unknowable God.

• Roger Hamm: **Stories, language, and children**

Jumping *in medius* (and we are always in the middle of the story), I find myself agreeing with Bruce very deeply, although, as a recovering academic, the language sometimes gets in the way. But as a storyteller, I applaud!

Postmodernism is not a system of belief, but a term attempting to define what

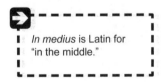

In medius is Latin for "in the middle."

is happening/has been happening in the world around us: an observation rather than a prescription. We turn to words to describe how the world turns: but we do have to be careful (or perhaps it's just me) that the words don't get in the way of what we are saying and doing. A short "Chelm" story to illustrate: A chelmnik was crawling along the path in the centre of the village. A passerby asked what he was doing. The chelmnik replied that he had lost a ruble—an entire ruble—and that he was searching for it. The passerby asked if he knew where he lost it. The chelmnik replied that if he knew that, it wouldn't be lost. "No," responded the passerby, "what general area did you lose the ruble?" "In my house," says the chelmnik. "But if you lost it in your house," says the incredulous passerby, "why are you looking out here on the path?" "In my house, it's dark!," says the chelmnik, "Out here, it's light!"

Too often we step into the light of "academia" and don't even realize that the dark place we raced out of is where we need to be.

I find Bruce's comments about prelinguistic children in relation to language/culture-oriented adults to be particularly interesting. . . . Interestingly, stories are an essential element of learning as a child; and the child's mind continually places itself into the centre of whatever story is being told. It is as a storyteller that I find the deepest and most satisfying connections both with children and with adults. As a believer, it is when I see evidence of God in my story (or of me in God's story) that I deepen and grow in my faith.

• Paula Spurr: **Post/Modern transitions**

Bear with me. I am not an academic, but an artist, and my thoughts tend to fly in all directions. It seems to me that at this moment in time postmodern thought is a reaction to modernity, like "We didn't like this, so instead we'll think that." In other words, we are in a time of transition, but we have not yet arrived at a new form of thought. Times of transition, like birth or death, are startling! They can be terrifying! We can be expected to have doubts and confusion about where we are going. But a little baby in the birth canal can dig its heels in all it wants, it will still be born; we can fight against our death with all our will, but we will not be able to stop the change coming upon us. Is this what is happening to us and the way we think and view the world?

Over the last fifteen years or so, I have found my worldview and thought system changing. I have often wondered if I was all alone in my dislike for the way the church approaches me and my culture (the world I live in). It is only in the last five years that I have begun reading and hearing about postmodern thought, and the thing that amazes me most is the validation of my thought processes. My mind has not been changed by learning about postmodernism.

. . . So we can talk about reason and mystery and think one thing or the other, but I believe "the times, they are a-changin'." Surely I am not the only dummy in this world who is unsatisfied with a modern approach to God. I want God to be more than a scientific formula, I am comforted to contemplate that his ways are far above my ways, I want my walk with God to be much more than a four-step recipe, and I know I am not the only one.

To me, this whole conversation is an attempt to ease the birthing process, to refer to my previous analogy. As any baby will tell you, leaving the comfort of the womb (modernity) is no fun, the trip through the birth canal (postmodernity) can be painful—but life itself (who knows what the new way of thinking will be?) is worth the journey.

- Myron Bradley Penner: **Postmodernism, authority, and moral absolutes**

I have greatly appreciated and benefited from Bruce Benson's work on postmodern thought, and this blog entry is no different. I think it orients the ensuing conversation to the postmodern phenomenon in a clear and helpful manner.

To begin with, the emphasis on seeing postmodernism as an attitude, instead of a position, is important if we are to understand and engage postmodernity. My own preference is to describe postmodernism as an **ethos**, as this reminds us that postmodernity (and modernity) is a kind of intellectual and spiritual posture or set of dispositions—not unlike a worldview—which orients its adherents toward the world in a particular manner and acts as a starting point for reflection. Too often those who wish to "refute" postmodernity make the (modern) mistake of trying to reduce it to a philosophical position. Rather than a set of philosophical theses or a particular methodology, the shift to postmodernity originates in an existential, "gut" reaction to the excesses of the modern ethos. Whatever else postmoderns are about—and they are about a wide variety of

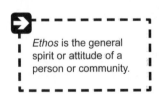
Ethos is the general spirit or attitude of a person or community.

things—they are unanimous in their refusal (or better, inability) to see the world as modernity suggests. Given its character as an ethos or attitude, disputing with postmodernity would more fruitfully take a dialogical form, as a better way to voice one's concerns about postmodernity by directly engaging its concerns, debates, and the basic conditions under which it flourishes.

Bruce also helpfully narrates the philosophical disagreement between moderns and postmoderns as rooted in different conceptions of the nature of human beings. This is probably the most important philosophical point upon which postmoderns will generally agree. The optimism of modernity stems from its notion of the autonomous self. Postmodernity's rejection of the modern self as a construction has profound consequences on human reason and knowledge, as Bruce recounts for us. Those who wish to dispute with modernity must take especial note of Bruce's entirely correct and crucial distinction between **epistemological** and **metaphysical** forms of **antirealism**. What postmodernists like Rorty and Derrida regularly deny is the ability of humans to re-present the "real" world fully in our concepts and language so as to constitute a firm and certain foundation for indubitable beliefs. But this is not necessarily the same as a skeptical denial of "knowledge," or a relativistic rejection of "truth," or a **nihilistic** negation of "value." In other words, accepting a version of epistemological antirealism in which our concepts of truth and knowledge are never taken as a **mimetic** re-presenting of reality as it really is, apart from our perceiving or thinking or speaking of it, does not commit one to metaphysical antirealism, according to which the "real world" does not exist

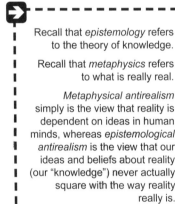

Recall that *epistemology* refers to the theory of knowledge.

Recall that *metaphysics* refers to what is really real.

Metaphysical antirealism simply is the view that reality is dependent on ideas in human minds, whereas *epistemological antirealism* is the view that our ideas and beliefs about reality (our "knowledge") never actually square with the way reality really is.

Nihilism is the view that there is no positive meaning or value in the universe.

Mimetic comes from the Greek word *memesis*, which essentially means "mirror."

independently of those who perceive it or think it or speak of it. The postmodern concern primarily is with epistemological, not metaphysical, realism.

Another powerful and illuminating way to narrate the story of the shifts from premodernity to modernity to postmodernity, though, is to **emplot** it around changing conceptions of authority. Descartes makes it abundantly clear that the transformation in philosophy he is recommending is first and foremost an issue of authority.[1] The traditional, external forms of authority accepted in premodernity left too much room for doubt. The only place, Descartes reasons, that one can possibly find immunity from doubt is within the "tranquility" and "solitude" of one's own mind.[2] With this internalization of reason (as opposed to the external *logos* of his medieval and ancient predecessors), Descartes effectively shifts the onus for rational belief onto individuals, who are now responsible to establish for themselves, and from within their own cognitive resources, the absolute and certain foundations for his or her knowledge—an assumption that serves the rest of modern philosophy. In other words, post-Descartes rational belief and action is a little like the evangelical conception of saving faith: rational beliefs and actions cannot be inherited and no one else can make them rational for you. The final court of appeal in all matters philosophical and theological (or political, for that matter) is reconceived as a form of human reason to which all (civilized) human beings have access, can all agree upon, and is the same for all (read: universal and objective). Thus the modern quest for the Theory of Everything begins.

> To *emplot* is to take a series of events and put them into a story that has a plot.

On this account, postmodernity involves a fundamental denial of the supremacy of human reason to act as an authority for human belief. But take careful note that this is a dispute with a particular conception of human reason and not a flat-out denial of the value of rational discourse. It is at this point in the story that postmoderns typically make the point, emphasized by Bruce in relation to Lyotard's "incredulity toward metanarratives," that rational justification and just human sense-making in general takes place within our narrative accounts of the world; and these narratives (and especially the modern metannarative) themselves are part of a wider ethos that involves a complex array of commitments, goals, and desires. That is, reasons and reason-giving are always made in the context of something like faith.

There is one aspect of Bruce's little story about postmodernism that gives me slight pause, and about which I would like to hear more from him. He tells us that, "Mediation by language in no way means that there cannot be 'direct' experience. I can still 'directly' perceive something. Yet, since that perception itself is always affected by categories of thought and thus language, then there is still mediation." So far, so good. I am in agreement. Of course, a large red cardinal can appear on the horizon of my phenomenal field just as it is, so to speak. It is my conceptualizing of it as "a large red cardinal" that is indirect and mediated. And while Bruce is quite right to note that in principle the variance in **semantic** and conceptual categories across cultures and languages are "neither absolute nor unbridgeable," I wonder about his

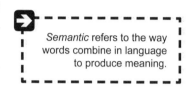

Semantic refers to the way words combine in language to produce meaning.

example of honoring one's parents as a cross-cultural universal that is instantiated in various ways. I do not want to contest the empirical universality of the honoring parents' phenomenon, rather I want to inquire into the nature of this "universal."

Is Bruce saying that this is a good ol' fashioned metaphysical property (or moral intuition) that operates as a timeless truth for moral evaluation? It seems to me that we do not have to resort to a modern framework to account for this—and I do not think Bruce is necessarily doing that. He just does not say more about it. I would view the confluence of certain moral principles across times and cultures/languages (and there are others in addition to honoring parents) to be due to the fact that humans exist in a similar environment, with roughly the same humanoid forms, and therefore have very similar forms of life. However, it seems that the work of Michel Foucault, and some of the moral experimentation that has gone on in twentieth-century pop culture, has given us some empirical evidence that indicates one can (at least in principle) deny these things and at least attempt to live as if there truly were no such universals. My point is not that these people falsify Christian moral norms, but that these norms make no sense and do not function as "universals" outside of a fundamental agreement with certain aspects of our narrative.

WHAT IS A POSTMODERN EVANGELICAL?

Myron Bradley Penner

Trying to define a "postmodern evangelical" is undoubtedly a fool's errand. Bruce Benson notes in his blog, "What Is 'Postmodernism'?" that there is no such thing as "postmodernism," so it is an audacious act indeed to attempt to articulate how an evangelical Christian could also be "postmodern." And there's no telling what an "evangelical" is these days either. The appellation may mean anything from "I believe in the divine, infallible, inerrant *interpretation* of Scripture"—as a freshman theology student of mine once wrote (mistakenly, I hope) in a theology paper—to "I vote Republican" or "I only listen to CCM (Contemporary Christian Music) and took a vow to remain a virgin until marriage." In fact, during the run-up to the 2004 US presidential election, Jerry Falwell declared on National Public Radio (http://www.npr.org/templates/story/story.php?storyId=3354001) that Jim Wallis, the founding editor of *Sojourners* magazine, was "as much an evangelical as an oak tree" simply because Wallis pointed out that the Republican Party does not have a monopoly on public morality in the United States (e.g., opposition to gay marriage) and that some of the platforms of the Democratic Party, such as overcoming poverty and protecting the environment, are values issues as well.

There is, of course, more to evangelicalism than the above caricatures—just as there is more to postmodernism than an absence of theory (see the rest of Bruce's blog for proof positive)—but they do highlight the difficulty in defining what an evangelical is. We may, however, distinguish between a prescriptive theological-historical characterization of evangelicalism and a more descriptive sociological categorization. As interesting as it would be to mount an exploration of the latter, more descriptive version, with its focus on the wider social practices and attitudes of the self-identified evangelical subculture, my focus here is not on this aspect of evangelicalism. In that regard I will simply note that North American evangelical subculture—with its televised programs and church services; its theme parks, bumper stickers, and like paraphernalia; and its ability to turn anything remotely related to Christianity into a consumer product—is waiting for a sustained sociological-theological analysis in terms of Jean Baudrillard's categories as a nihilistic fixation on **simulacra** and **hyperreality**. Perhaps we North American evangelicals need to question the degree to which we performatively pronounce the death of God through the media of our subculture and thereby lose our ability to profess the gospel in our wider culture—despite the slogans we put through the airwaves, in our tracts, and onto our billboards.

> *Simulacrum* refers to something that bears resemblance to a real object and stands in its place.
>
> *Hyperreality* refers to technologically enhanced reality, which eventually takes the place of "normal" reality. For example, pornography and virtual sex may replace physical sexual interaction.
>
> *Transdenomonational* means "across churches of different denominations."
>
> *Geist* is a German word meaning "spirit" or "mind."
>
> *Pietism* generally refers to personal attention to spiritual practice.

Whatever the case may be, I am more concerned with the theological-historical version. While it is a **transdenominational** movement, with various styles and forms, we may think of the diverse expressions of evangelicalism as exhibiting what Ludwig Wittgenstein called "family resemblances."[1] The key, both etymologically and historically, to understanding the wide variety of evangelicals (and evangelicalisms) is their central preoccupation with the *evangel*—the "Good News" of the gospel of Jesus Christ—in terms of its normative truth and the necessity of its proclamation.[2] To oversimplify, the evangelical focus on the gospel has led to two poles within the evangelical *geist*, with individual evangelical communities gravitating in greater or lesser degrees to one pole or the other.[3] There is, on one hand, a **pietistic** and devotional pole, which emphasizes the personal, activist elements of Christian faith such as conversion (i.e., being "born again"), sharing one's faith (evangelism), and devotional uses of Scripture (reading, memorizing, meditating, etc.), and finds its roots in the evangelical revivals of the eighteenth and nineteenth centuries. On the other hand, there is a theological emphasis on doctrinal correctness, especially on Scripture as the **inerrant** and authoritative Word of God, which stems from a reaction against modern liberal attacks on the authority of Scripture and the subsequent doctrinal revisions that followed.[4] In keeping with this bipolar nature of evangelicalism, evangelicals have been identified interchangeably as "born again Christians" who have accepted Jesus into their hearts, or "fundamentalists" who believe in the doctrine of the inerrancy of Scripture.[5]

Thus the present-day evangelical concern for the gospel has a history: it emerges in modernity, within the modern cultural and philosophical context, due to the variety of social and cultural factors that shaped modernism, and is therefore mediated by the concerns, categories, and concepts of modernity. As a result, evangelicalism has a distinctly modern flavor. In this regard it is difficult to overestimate the significance that modern **higher biblical criticism** and the subsequent rise of modern theological liberalism has had in shaping the contours of modern evangelical identity. Modern liberalism, with its wholesale adoption of modern assumptions regarding the authority of universal

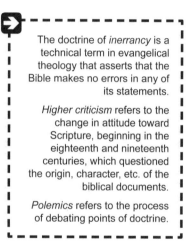

The doctrine of *inerrancy* is a technical term in evangelical theology that asserts that the Bible makes no errors in any of its statements.

Higher criticism refers to the change in attitude toward Scripture, beginning in the eighteenth and nineteenth centuries, which questioned the origin, character, etc. of the biblical documents.

Polemics refers to the process of debating points of doctrine.

and autonomous human reason, negatively defines evangelicalism in the twentieth century: whatever else we are, we evangelicals are *not liberal*. By and large, liberalism regarded the Scriptures as authoritative only insofar as they agreed with the dictates of human reason (natural revelation), and liberal theological method was one of correlation between the categories of theology and those of modern culture and philosophy.

It is in this context, over and against modern liberalism, that evangelicalism sought to articulate and defend the gospel of Jesus to at least four effects (there are many more):

1. Evangelical theology has had a distinct apologetic and **polemical**

character, concerned with defending the rationality of evangelical truth claims from the external attacks of secular atheistic naturalism, and defending historic orthodox doctrine from attacks within. Thus evangelical thought has been preoccupied with gatekeeping, if you will. There has been a need to distinguish those who are "in," included in evangelicalism, from those who are "out."

2. In order to accomplish the apologetic and polemical tasks, evangelicalism has focused on doctrinal correctness and the **propositional** aspects of the gospel. In other words, the gospel is understood to consist of identifiable propositions that have been revealed from God in Scripture and are absolutely true and rationally defensible. Renowned evangelical theologian Carl Henry goes so far as to say that *all* of God's revelation is aimed at transmitting propositional truths and the goal of Scripture, therefore, is the communication of such truths regardless of its diverse literary forms.[6] Thus in modernity an unholy divorce occurs, in which evangelicals come to understand the gospel almost exclusively in terms of its propositional and doctrinal dimension, whereas liberals interpreted the gospel in social and ethical terms almost to the exclusion of its cognitive elements.

The term *proposition* refers to what is asserted in a declarative sentence. In this case, *propositional* refers to whatever is stated in language.

Historically, *positivism* refers to the idea that every true statement can be verified scientifically.

3. The above, in turn, led to a kind of apologetic **positivism** in evangelicalism, according to which the gospel and Scripture are treated reductively as authoritative if (and only if) one has marshaled enough evidence or presuppositional coherence to establish its rationality (as conceived in modernity).

4. There is also in modern evangelicalism a strong emphasis on individualism that accompanies its stress on personal response to the gospel. In keeping with this, the doctrine of the church is

emaciated, as interpreting Scripture and just the spiritual life in general is conceived as mostly a solitary experience.

The degree to which evangelicals accept the postmodern turn is the degree to which they are able to recognize this historically situated evangelical identity and will seek to frame the evangelical emphasis on the gospel in other terms. I want to suggest that one may be committed to the gospel of Jesus Christ and at the same time accept a general critique of the modern categories through which evangelism frames its understanding of the gospel. Some evangelicals—call them "postconservative," "postevangelical," "emergent," or whatever term you prefer—feel they can no longer express their faith in terms set down by traditional evangelicalism, not because they disagree with those terms but because those terms simply fail to express adequately their convictions borne of careful reflection on Scripture and their experiences of walking with Christ. The trouble, as postmodern evangelicals see it, is that evangelicalism itself does not escape the modernist net. Put simply, the postmodern evangelicals I am describing often find the issues and concerns addressed by the theologies of their evangelical forbearers to answer and address questions they are not asking—questions, methods, and answers which arise from a fundamentally modernist conceptual paradigm.

In what sense, though, can an evangelicalism at all worthy of that name survive postmodern suspicion? It all depends, first, upon what you mean by "postmodernism" and then, second, on what you are calling "evangelical." If by "postmodernism" you mean a **nihilistic** form of **epistemic** and moral **relativism,** then not much that is evangelical (and just not much period) will survive in postmodernity. However, I believe that postmodernism is much

Nihilism, epistemology, and relativism were all defined in Blog 1.

more nuanced than this one form of it (again, see Bruce Benson's blog on "What Is 'Postmodernism'?"). And if by evangelicalism you mean *modern* evangelicalism, then again not much that is evangelical can be expressed in a postmodern context. An evangelical emphasis—placing a priority on the gospel of Jesus Christ—in a postmodern context will necessarily be understood differently than modern evangelicalism. But it will not be unrecognizable, nor will it be completely different. (And why would it be? Modernism and postmodernism cannot be differentiated absolutely either.) In fact, a postmodern evangelicalism will have broadly the same basic shape to it as in modernity—for example, the centrality of Jesus Christ and the emphases on personal piety and the authority of Scripture. It will continue to emphasize what we might call the "basics" of the gospel, or what C. S. Lewis called "mere Christianity." The difference is that these basics will be reconfigured and understood through categories that are not modern.

Ultimately there cannot be *one* "postmodern evangelicalism" but a variety of ways of being evangelical in a postmodern context, each of which are centered around the faithful proclamation of the gospel of Jesus Christ. There will be some ambiguities around the edges of such a community, but not an absolute abandonment of the ability to determine who's "in" and who's "out": some are definitely in, others definitely out, but for a small group we will not know what to say and will have to exercise godly discernment. The more important point is that saying who's "in" and who's "out" is not as high of a priority for evangelicals in a postmodern context as it has been. Furthermore, for postmodern evangelicals apologetics does not occupy the same role; doctrine is closely connected to the concrete practices connected to the church's proclamation of the gospel; and the church universal as the community called together by the Holy Spirit is paramount to the wider aspects of Christian life, including our biblical interpretation and theological reflections.

COMMENTS

THREAD ONE:
LABELS, STORIES, AND IDENTITIES

- AI: **Defining "evangelical" and "postmodern"**

For my taste, two definitions of "evangelical" are most helpful. First, in a 1998 article in the Australian Evangelical Alliance periodical *Working Together*, World Evangelical Alliance statesman Leon Morris wrote [that an evangelical is, by definition, someone concerned with the gospel]. This means more than just preaching the gospel now and then; it means that for him or her the gospel of Christ is central. The gospel is an evangelical's message and he or she preaches it, constantly. But it is more than a subject of preaching: the gospel is at the centre of that person's thinking and living. Second, in 2003, Ipsos-Reid Corporation surveyed some 3,000 Canadians to seek improved understanding of Canada's evangelical community. Among the findings was the estimate that 19 percent of Canadians (some 6 million) can be regarded as "evangelical" (12 percent Protestant and 7 percent Catholic) on the basis of respondents' replies to six key criteria. These criteria included agreement with the following statements:

1. I believe that through the life, death and resurrection of Jesus, God provided the way for the forgiveness of my sins;

2. I believe the Bible to be the word of God and is reliable and trustworthy; and

3. I have committed my life to Christ and consider myself to be a converted Christian.

Next, to be counted as "evangelical" respondents needed to disagree with these statements:

4.   The concept of God is an old superstition that is no longer needed to explain things in these modern times; and

5.   In my view, Jesus Christ was not the divine Son of God.

The sixth criterion for being counted as an "evangelical" was respondents' weekly church attendance.

These six criteria may be more sociological than theological, but at least they offer some relatively useful understanding of the term "evangelical," at least in my opinion. (Note that this 2003 survey replicated a similar survey a decade previous.)

For my taste, virtually all definitions of "postmodern" that I have read in the past decade or two are much less helpful than the above two approaches to defining "evangelical." Virtually all of them note that we now live in "postmodern" times, though I often wonder whether even 1 percent of the world's population have any sense of that. I wonder whether even 1 percent of citizens of Europe and North America have any sense of that, and whether even 10 percent of those citizens of Europe and North America who hold a postsecondary degree of any sort have any grasp of this notion. Those intelligentsia who attempt to define postmodernism often allude to the political and perspectival nature of language and to the impact of our communities on our worldview beliefs and behaviours, yet both of these observations are at least as old as Francis Bacon (1561–1626). These same intelligentsia also note how **pomos** repudiate "modernism," [but their rejection of modernism as] some exaggerated optimism regarding the powers of human reason to deliver **apodictically** certain knowledge [is] likely not representative of many humans other than rationalists such as R. Descartes, G. W. Leibniz, B. Spinoza, C. Wolff, and their disciples.

> *Pomo* = "postmodern"
>
> *Apodictic* refers to something that can be proven to be true with absolute certainty.

For me, such definitions of "postmodernism" usually raise the suspicion that some people are trying to invent a new "language-game" which might serve primarily as an elite Gnosticism whose intent is to distinguish themselves as intelligentsia who are obviously much wiser than the common rabble of laity [surveyed in] the 2003 Ipsos-Reid survey.

Does this pomo language-game generate a new professional-laity divide that may be as counterproductive to the ministry of the Christian gospel as was the Jew-Gentile division at Galatia? Does this pomo language-game betray an idolatry of novelty, so often characteristic of intelligentsia of all worldviews? Is this discussion really primarily another philosophical fad that is liable to pass from the philosophical scene as quickly as did **existentialism**, likely its precursor?

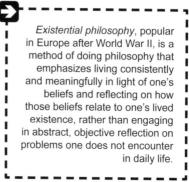

Existential philosophy, popular in Europe after World War II, is a method of doing philosophy that emphasizes living consistently and meaningfully in light of one's beliefs and reflecting on how those beliefs relate to one's lived existence, rather than engaging in abstract, objective reflection on problems one does not encounter in daily life.

Virtually all definitions of "postmodern evangelical" I have read in the past decade or two strike me as even less helpful than the separate definitions of "postmodern" and "evangelical," and that for mostly the same reasons. Dr. Penner's post and the discussion it has generated have not dissipated my skepticism in this matter. I wonder how many of Canada's estimated 6 million evangelicals would relate in any meaningful fashion with this discussion. I might ask the same concerning the estimated 40–50 million American evangelicals. I might ask the same concerning the untold millions of evangelicals (mostly laity) around the world who faithfully live and proclaim our Lord's evangel in terms very relevant to themselves and their neighbours.

Does anyone on this blog share such concerns?

- Eric Mason: **A story of how labels (do not) define me**

Al: I count myself an evangelical. I am also distinctly postmodern in my worldview. I only use the term "postmodern" to define what I am not. Postmodernism must be seen as something that is emerging from modernism. Defining "evangelical" is fairly simple. I just look it up. But even then, Dr. Morris' statement for the

WEA is fairly nebulous (http://www.worldevangelicalalliance.com/wea/evangelical.htm).

I'm glad. I read it with great joy. I could be an evangelical by the other survey-style definition as well, but Dr. Morris' statement is much more open and generous. The things is, it would be a distinctly modern desire to want to nail down a definition of postmodern. "Postmodernism" is as yet a very broad term to describe things arising (or, in some cases, descending) from modernism. It's like trying to sum up everything that has happened to you since your birth in a single sentence. You could say, "I grew up." That would be correct, but it surely wouldn't define you. God forbid that someone try to box me up in a single definition that I would have to adhere to. (If I accepted labeling so easily I might not have a postmodern worldview.) But then again, I love my labels too. I am a Texan, who lives in Indiana, and is moving to Colorado. I am an actor/writer, a pastor/teacher, a leader/follower/father/husband.

> WEA = World Evangelical Alliance
>
> *Animism* literally refers to the religious practice of attributing supernatural powers and beings to material objects (e.g., trees, water, rocks, etc.). Here it may also refer to the practice of ritual sacrifice that often accompanies animistic religion.

I have worked full-time variously as a theater director, actor, pit crew member, trapeze performer, factory worker, waiter, web designer, and English teacher. I have ministered full-time in Reformed, Baptist, fundamentalist, Willowish, and Catholic settings. I am an evangelical. I love my labels. Yet I demand I am the labeler.

I'm not sure that there is or will be a "helpful" definition for "postmodern." I'm not sure why it's important to have one. I agree wholeheartedly that there are distinctly bad things descending from modernism (a return to pagan **animism,** for example). There are numerous positive things arising from postmodernism (greater diversity and a recovery of ancient Christian practices, for example). I also believe that if the local Christian church in the West wishes to thrive, it will need to be more and more postmodern in its practice and teaching. I also [believe] that postmodernism will pass away and that not one idea but a multitude of ideas and practices will emerge, perhaps as various as our geographies.

- AI: **Who I am: An evangelical story**

For the sake of Eric and others who may have an interest in a narrative of my journey, it may be worthwhile for me to share (selectively, of course), [in light of this] "new kind of conversation," what it means to be a "postmodern evangelical." I'll group my thoughts into the following three broader topics: 1) who I am, 2) what I've done, and 3) how I feel.

1) Who I am: I see myself as created in God's image, but a fallen sinner saved by God's grace through the atoning sacrifice of the God-man Jesus Christ who was sent to be my Savior (incarnation, **substitutionary death**, resurrection and ascension to glory, and coming to take us to glory to spend eternity with him). I see myself as seeking to be a radical disciple, serving Christ in everything I do to his greater glory and to the strengthening and extension of his church through the power of his Word and his Holy Spirit.

> *Substitutionary atonement* refers to the belief that Jesus took our place on the cross and suffered on our behalf—as a "substitute" sacrifice for our sin.

2) What I've done: Besides teaching high school (mostly math and science) three years and directing a Bible camp for eight years, some forty years of teaching Sunday school and various preaching opportunities, mostly in churches, camps, and some conferences, teaching in a Bible college some twenty-eight years and in a seminary full-time seven years and part-time some dozen years, I've helped numerous Bible colleges and seminaries achieve accreditation and written a bunch of articles on a variety of topics and a book on the Bible college movement in Canada. Some years ago the local chapter of Sigma Xi (a fraternity of research scientists) invited me to share with them my views on earth-life origins and what should be done in public education on this matter in dialogue with a committed evolutionist who teaches at a local university. I helped launch a Christian liberal arts college in the former Soviet Union shortly after the fall of communism (primarily its academic dimensions) and directed a seminary branch campus in India in partnership with a local indigenous mission agency at their invitation, including teaching there on three occasions. I've studied at Three Hills (Alberta), Winnipeg, Chicago, and New York, besides living in Manitoba, Saskatchewan, and Arkansas. And in my numerous dialogues with people who are either largely

unaware of or antagonistic to the Christian message of salvation, postmodernism has never been an issue in any part of the world.

3) How I feel, particularly concerning the postmodern evangelical "conversation": I have mostly felt despised as a "modernist," particularly as a "polemicist," particularly in my role as a professor of theology and philosophy, including teaching apologetics and ethics. I am well past the stage of teen rebellion against the church and its weaknesses, which have sadly been a part of Christ's bride in every generation since New Testament times. The music of the **"emerging church"** and its theological fuzziness is not exhilarating to me—as it may be to Gen-Xers who seem excessively fixated on novelty, [which] is characteristic of adolescents. I have likely never suffered such a personal diatribe as I received from a postmodern evangelical over a year ago, when he did not like my critique of an article he was preparing for publication and had invited my prepublication critique. What I think will make the evangelical church thrive is not some vague tinkering with the vague **shibboleths** of the "postmodern evangelical" or "emerging church" in-group language-game. Instead, I think what will make the evangelical church thrive is a radical discipleship to the biblical commitments called for in Rick Warren's "Purpose-Driven Life." **IMHO, Brian McLaren** and his disciples have much to learn from the latter.

The *emerging church* is a loose collection of Christians (mostly in North America, Western Europe, Africa, and the South Pacific) who believe the traditional church, with its theological and organizational structures, has been sidetracked by modernity, and subsequently seek to explore alternative ("postmodern") expressions of Christianity.

A *shibboleth* is a word or catch phrase members of a group use to distinguish their members from others (outsiders).

IMHO = "in my humble opinion"

Brian McLaren's writings are often looked to by members of the emerging church as articulating a theology that is relevant for our postmodern times.

That is a summary narrative of my personal journey, though I recognize that it is quite different from the personal journeys of Gen-Xers who seek "a new kind of conversation" via this blog. Frankly, I feel alienated by all the vitriol against "modernism," especially when that straw man is left largely undefined as the bogeyman of postmodernism. As such, I fail to see much "conversation" on this site—mostly too much self-congratulation that "we postmodernists" are not like those poor benighted "modernists" who still feel the need to seek understanding of what the Christian gospel actually means in itself and how it is to be lived and proclaimed in every culture around the world and in every generation.

. . . I might now add that part of the personal diatribe from which I still hurt was the dismissive judgment: "You don't understand and don't want to." When one sincerely is asking for clarification, such "postmodern evangelical" judgments are singularly unhelpful, though I have not seen a submission on this blog from the author of that comment.

I might now also add that, though I grew up in an independent Mennonite church that was primarily committed to missions and therefore soon joined the Evangelical Free Church, my ministerial/pastoral services have been both in a more traditional Mennonite church and in an Evangelical Free Church in New York City. . . .

Does anyone on this site resonate with these perspectives?

- Eric Mason: **Do we need to define what a "postmodern evangelical" is?**

I resonate, man. I'm currently a pastor to students in an Evangelical Free church in a Mennonite and Amish area (Elkhart County, Indiana). But I'm a tad younger, I think.

Why do we need to define "postmodernism"? Why do we need to define "postmodern evangelical"? The term simply means an evangelical who is emerging from many of the tenets of modernism. Trying to define it is in many ways the "fool's errand" that Dr. Penner describes, because the nature of a postmodern evangelical can be any number of things and can be something different tomorrow. Here's a fun analogy that moves this to the mainstream.

In many ways, I could see this like the current conflict between Jack and Locke in the American television series *Lost*. Locke the shaman/hunter and Jack the scientist/realist/hero battle over issues of indiscernible actualities. Locke pressures Jack to simply act on faith without knowledge; Jack refuses to act without a rational explanation. Just a thought. Al, don't take this the wrong way. The shaman Locke is often erratic and chaotic and misguided. He often appears frustrated and wild. Jack seems empty and hard. He lacks transcendence. They both have their challenges and they are more alike than they are different.

- Greg McRitchie: **Modernism in the church?**

Good points, Al. I have many of the same concerns that you do and am glad you have stated them so cogently. I have seen many valid observations/criticisms of the current state of evangelicalism here and some I take great exception to, such as the supposed modernism in the church. (Can we get some specific examples?) I am also very concerned, as you are, about the vagueness of the solutions being put forth as a remedy. They seem to resonate (at least methodologically) with liberalism and mysticism. This is very disconcerting. If the concern is for mission, then these types of answers would seem to kill, not reinvigorate, missions.

- Jonathan Wood: **Who am I? A *postmodern* evangelical story**

Al, thanks for the narrative; it is very helpful in understanding who you are. I will take the liberty of apologizing for everyone here if you have felt alienated in this conversation because of your particular stance. I don't think it is intentional; as a brother in Christ we are essentially linked in bone and ligament, and nothing can change that.

Let me tell you my story. I grew up in a Christian home under wonderful Christian parents who taught me more about "Christianity" than all my later theological training taught me. However, when I moved out of the home I fell into drug addiction and other entrapping sins. When I finally decided to break from this lifestyle, I moved to Montana to attend a one-year fundamentalist Bible school. At this school I was taught to read and interpret the Bible according to modern **hermeneutical** methods and modern philosophical presuppositions. I learned a lot and excelled in this program. However, when I left the school and went into the mission field I found myself in deep crisis. Once again I dealt with drug addiction and other old habitual sins. I felt completely powerless

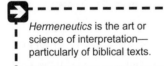

Hermeneutics is the art or science of interpretation—particularly of biblical texts.

over my own life. It was not that I wasn't trying to break with the old and put on the new man; it was just that I had a theological and philosophical framework that distracted me from the real issues underlying my crisis.

The following year was the most spiritual testing that I have ever had. Eventually I came to a despairing point where I recognized that, despite my "mastery" of doctrine, God was less of a reality in my life than he ever was. I believe that this was essentially linked to the concise, systematic definitions of God that I had been taught (and the consequential eradication of so much mystery that I needed in my conception of God). I had never been taught that there is a strict separation between knowing about God and knowing God. I came to a point where I realized I had to completely, in dreadful humility, let go of my theology if I wanted to return to the God who speaks through Holy Scripture. All of my theological and philosophical training since has been tempered by this experience, this **existential understanding** that ultimately the appeal to knowledge can be the antithesis of faith.

> An "existential understanding" is the sort of thing one understands by doing (or being) something, as opposed to merely thinking about it or having it explained by someone else.

For this reason postmodern philosophy and theology resonates much more strongly to me (and many of my colleagues): not that it gets me any closer to God than modern philosophy and theology, but because it continually critiques those things that we think we know—making more room for consciousness of the infinite demand that faith places on me at every moment. I understand that my experience in a particular fundamentalism does not represent all modern Christian paradigms. However, I personally believe (from my own experience) that modernism in general is subject to many of these same tendencies. I believe that if I am to be faithful to God as I have heard him speak in the Scriptures, tradition, and my own life, I must speak against and warn others of those things that I have experienced as snares in my own life.

- Myron Bradley Penner: **Identity, story, and body**

It is great to have some of you share your stories. Stories are crucial to forming and shaping who we are, and to helping others identify who we are. I think in many ways the stories offered here do a better job of "explaining" what I am talking about than my blog post, as they embody the narratives of those of us having this conversation. I trust that all of us have a clearer picture what is going on in this conversation, and what is at stake in it, through reading and interacting with these stories. (BTW: I too have a Mennonite background!)

Two quick comments. First, Al, I would like also to express my regret over and condemnation of the sort of self-righteous, judgmental attitude you describe. I trust that you have not experienced this reading my entries; but if you have, please know that this has never been my intended spirit and please accept my sincere apology. I am, however, a little puzzled by your apparent dismissal of my discussion of postmodern evangelicalism, as I explicitly reference both the theological and the sociological approaches you find so helpful! I am very glad to see that we both place the evangel front and center in our understanding of evangelicalism. It appears to me that we have quite a lot in common; certainly enough from which to continue fruitful conversation and mutual understanding.

Second, I'd like to roundly endorse something Eric said, and connect it to a point Jonathan made. Eric is correct, in my view, to point out that those of us who are exploring postmodern ways of being evangelical share a fundamental identity with those who are traditionally (modern) evangelical. Beyond the sociological connection of both camps belonging to the same community (while occupying different factions within it), the deeper reality (as Jonathan points out) is that we are connected "bone and ligament" (I like that phrase—it calls to mind Miguel de Unamuno's "Man of Flesh and Bone") in the body of Christ. That is the bottom line in this discussion. Our blessed hope is that one day these stories of ours— with all their differences, frustrations, and misunderstandings—will culminate in a shared ending at Christ's return that wraps up all the loose ends and rabbit trails. In the end, our story, each and all of ours, will be "his-story."

THREAD TWO:
MODERNISM AND EVANGELICAL CHRISTIANITY

- Warren McCaig: **Evangelical ministry and post/modernism**

Greg, in your earlier post [above] you stated [that you wanted specific examples of modernism in the evangelical church].

Certainly I cannot speak authoritatively on behalf of anyone else and their concerns about the marriage of the church and the philosophical framework of modernity. What I will attempt to do, however, is outline what I see as a few examples of this and why a number of people, myself included (call us postmodern, emergent, postcolonial, or what you will), want to move away from a framework that allows for and sometimes promotes this type of error.

1. A view of salvation that is based on gaining **epistemic certainty** about certain propositions pertaining to Christ and ourselves. Whether intentionally or not, the Western church has (to a large extent) embraced a view of salvation that is primarily concerned with changing an individual person's status in the eyes of God from sinner to saint. This change in status is enabled by the person affirming certain propositions, after which one can be assured that his or her eternal destination has changed and he or she is in right standing with God. This view of salvation does have valid aspects, but its wide-scale deployment has led to the **commoditization** of God's grace and likely (God will be the judge) the false assurance of thousands (millions?) of people, people who assume that by praying a certain prayer or repeating after a minister that their **justification** is complete. If God by his grace chooses to grant salvation to these people, the church has still succeeded in changing the life-transforming message of Christ and his ministry on earth to a personal atonement drive-through.

> *Epistemic certainty* refers here to our being able to prove our beliefs absolutely.
>
> *Commoditization* refers to the process of transforming something (in this case God's grace) into a consumer product that can be bought or sold.
>
> *Justification* is a theological term that refers to our being righteous— i.e., "justified" before God.

2. Christian interaction with society that is based on false (unjust) metanarratives. Christians in North America live in a unique situation, one where we feel that persecution is any civil action that does not promote our views and ethics in a position of dominance over the views of others (Justice Sunday anyone?). Married to our **consumerist** version of salvation is the view that the West's position of economic and global dominance in some way is based on divine reward for faithfulness or service. This view is responsible for an ethic that leaves Christians promoting the denial of civil liberties to those living in certain sins while allowing [other] sins to go unabated (a new kind of Pharisee perhaps?). At the same time, we promote wholeheartedly an economic system that favors the rich and neglects the poor (both on a national and international level). If that isn't bad enough, many times this gets combined with an **eschatology** that sees the West and its allies representing God against the world in the end of all things. Churches thoroughly baptized in this metanarrative have affirmed and given God's blessing to a government that neglects the genocide of peoples (Rwanda in the past, Sudan currently) while using questionable evidence to engage militarily with nations and for questionable motives. (Read Kenzo's blog [at the end of this chapter] to get a far more authoritative and well-researched look at how Christianity in the West is married to our historical and philosophical background.)

> *Consumerism* refers to a preoccupation with goods that can be bought or sold.
>
> *Eschatology* is the branch of theology that concerns the end of human history and human destiny.

These issues, along with many others, are the reasons I honestly look to engage new ideas and new conversations. I desire to be part of a church that holds more loosely to its defining propositions and more tightly to its defining actions.

. . . In realizing that I am at least to some extent lost or misguided in my views (and lacking the absolute aerial viewpoint), I prefer to write the first few maps in pencil, realizing that the landscape may look very different from any number of positions, altitudes, and angles. Consider that leaders who are asking questions like the kind you see in these discussions are for good reason hesitant to give concrete directions or positions. No one would want to be responsible for sending people an absolute map into a place where one cannot be fully certain of the territory and getting them more lost.

. . . You closed by saying [that you found all this] "very disconcerting," and that "if the concern is for mission, then [postmodern evangelical] answers would seem to kill, not reinvigorate, missions."

My own personal desire for involvement in ministry has been awakened and driven by the questions and suggestions of many of the thinkers who are involved with this blog. As I work in missions I strive to seek out how to bring Christ and his kingdom without forcing the embrace of modernist constructs.

• Greg McRitchie: **"Blind guides" of postmodernity**

Warren, you make some good points and I agree with you about the sorry state of the evangelical church at large in North America. I live in Canada, so there are some differences, but most of our churches seem to have succumbed to the seeker-sensitive, experiencing-God-for-forty-days or the prayer-of-Jabez, fad-of-the-week type things. Our grace is cheap and our gospel (when we bother to preach it) is weak because we fail to preach it clearly and don't seem to live it out. So I agree with much of your first point.

. . . I strongly disagree [with your point about writing provisional maps in pencil and avoiding absolute maps, which] I think runs right through your post. No one that I know argues for absolute certainty in all points of doctrine. If we were left to our own devices, I think you would be right: we would have to feel our way along and even then we would not know. God has given us his Word and the Spirit has illuminated it so that we do not have to be blind anymore. . . . If we are to adopt postmodernism's worldly, philosophical (and I might add unbiblical), skeptical approach to Scripture, then we will not be able to discern (know) anything. Our leaders will be but "blind guides." "And if the blind leads the blind, both will fall into a ditch" (Matthew 15:14 NKJV). I don't need pencil drawings to see where this leads.

. . . [This all seems a lot like liberalism, and] liberalism can be summed up in one word: disbelief. The social gospel is all social and no gospel. It fills men's bellies and damns their souls. We need [both to care for social problems *and* to preach the Word], but we will not be able to proclaim anything but personal stories that lack the power of the Spirit if we sabotage the certainty of the gospel through unwarranted skepticism. Notice the lack of the mention of sin on this site and you begin to see how this will play out.

. . . There is plenty of mystery in biblical Christianity, but the basis for our confession is not found in dreams and visions or "cunningly devised fables." Rather, it is found in the facts of the incarnation of the Son of God who came and lived a sinless life and then laid that life down as a substitutionary sacrifice for our sin and who **imputes** his righteousness to our account through faith *alone*. That's the message I am sure of. That's the "sure word" that saves sinners and transforms lives. That's a message you can preach in Bolivia or Bombay, in Kenya or Karachi. The Spirit works through the foolishness of preaching. And our success is measured in faithfulness to the Word, both in our preaching and in our lives. God bless you for serving him in missions.

> *Imputed righteousness* is a theological term that refers to our being declared or treated as righteous, not because we really are, but because Christ is righteous for us.

• Warren McCaig: **We need more liberal *concern*, not libera*lism*!**

. . . [Greg:] I resonate with your displeasure in the evangelical church in Canada and its love of the latest and greatest teaching. Having said that, I have a hard time understanding what alternative can be presented until evangelicals engage root issues that [lead to the problems you and I have identified. I see the main problem] as the strong marriage between the Western evangelical church and Western economic dominance, and the love that this has created for all things new and material.

. . . My primary confusion [over] your perspective [comes from the way you juxtapose our need for "absolute truth" and our lack of certainty and subsequent dependence on God's Spirit to be our guide]. I agree that the Holy Spirit has a primary role in our understanding of Scripture. Clearly, however (seen from a brief look at events in church history), this work of the Spirit does prevent the church, on a large scale, from promoting things that are contrary to the message of the kingdom that was promoted by Christ. [At the same time, the Spirit] has not and does not (and, I venture, does not attempt to) prevent the church from using the vernacular of both secular and religious philosophers to define and better understand itself.

. . . [I also have trouble with your statements about postmoderns adopting a "worldly philosophical" and "skeptical approach to Scripture" that only leads to blind leaders.] Here I have the same confusion that I mention above. . . . I fully understand the fear of being led by the blind and I also agree that some postmoderns will jettison the truth about Christ for a teaching of their [own] choosing. Unfortunately, I cannot find leaders anywhere who are philosophically nonsituated. I have a hard time knowing what church or ministry organization I could belong to that would hold *the* correct views (Jerry Falwell's? Pat Robertson's?). What church can I attend that has a theology that has not been influenced by [any of the] philosophical changes of the last 2,000 years? The last 200? You may not need a pencil drawing to see where we will end up with the blind leading the blind, [but I still] prefer to sketch with a pencil because all of us and those we follow are both partially blind and partially seeing. You may not see it this way, but I fail to see where we can [obtain] a nonsituated understanding of God or the Bible. . . . Christian views have been constantly adapting and changing since the first century. The work of the Holy Spirit does not counteract this.

You then go on to say that liberalism "fills men's bellies and damns their souls." Perhaps this is true with a wholesale acceptance of liberalism in its worst forms. What many on this site are looking for, myself included, is to borrow the concern that liberals have for people and their bellies (to use your terminology), to overcome a breed of Christianity that is far too happy with having overfilled its personal appetites at the expense of others. Many of the conservative leaders of Western Christianity promote views that, if followed to their conclusions, end up creating widows and orphans, or putting them to work. . . . This, and a Western Christian tendency (pointed out by Myron) to market everything (Anyone have a WWJD binder large enough to hold my *Left Behind* edition designed for middle children in families with over five members?), creates a belief system that needs an infusion—not an infusion of liberalism, but an infusion of the liberal concern for the needs and welfare of others.

I am not fully sure who you are referring to when you suggest that people on this blog are not willing to entertain the concept of sin. While I cannot speak for everyone, I do know personally a couple [contributors] and they [definitely] believe in sin and its consequences in the world. . . . [And i]n no way do I find my sense of passion for missions through a belief that there are many ways [to God], or that there is no need of salvation in the first place [as you imply]. Rather (to borrow from McLaren), I am excited to promote a Christ [who] is the way, but not *in* the way. Often I think we have to watch out that we are not making it more challenging to accept Christ than he made it.

. . . You regularly appeal to Scripture. . . . Whose interpretation of Scripture are you appealing to? How far separated from that view can one's perspective be before losing its value? If Christ is the only issue of importance, why do we teach anything else? If there is need for other teaching on issues, which commentary set do we use to arrive at correct conclusions? Maybe you can see what I am getting at here.

- Myron Bradley Penner: **Modern conversion and evangelism**

I'd like to say a hearty "Amen" to much of what Warren has said. I thought I had provided some fairly specific examples of ways North American evangelical subculture has capitulated to modernity, but Warren has filled out one side of that for me. Thanks.

THREAD THREE:
MISCELLANEOUS COMMENTS ON POSTMODERNISM
AND EVANGELICAL CHRISTIANITY

- Greg McRitchie: **Postmodernism is a form of liberalism**

[Myron,] you have rightly identified the true modernist Christians as those who elevated human reason above Scripture. What I can't understand is why you failed to notice that [modern Christians] are also the ones who moved into **existential philosophy** in an attempt to keep some semblance of the God whom they had destroyed through empty reasoning. [The postmodern evangelicalism] you are clearly advocating is nothing but the same methodology that led to the ruin of [liberal] clubs. **Machem** was right [when he said] that liberalism is a religion altogether distinct from biblical Christianity. . . . [Myron,] yours and those like you have formulated a recipe for disaster. It is unfaithfulness in its most damning form: deceitfulness. You can't have your cake and eat it too.

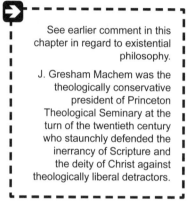

See earlier comment in this chapter in regard to existential philosophy.

J. Gresham Machem was the theologically conservative president of Princeton Theological Seminary at the turn of the twentieth century who staunchly defended the inerrancy of Scripture and the deity of Christ against theologically liberal detractors.

[Editors' comment: In fairness to Greg, we should add that he later apologized for this "uncharitable remark" and indicated that, after rereading Blog Two, even though he is convinced Myron is wrong he also believes "Dr. Penner has an honest and sincere desire to see the church (both individually and corporately) become a more faithful witness of Christ and him crucified to the culture of our day." Well done!]

- Richard Sudworth: **Postmodern evangelicalism and ecumenism**

Some great thoughts from Myron and ideas that make complete sense in the [British] context. I think there are additional implications for a postmodernism

The phrase "a high view of Scripture" typically refers to the belief in the authority of Scripture and its divine nature—i.e., that it is the Word of God and should be interpreted as his message to us.

evangelicalism in various guises with regard to unity and cross-fertilisation [*sic*] between [Christian] traditions. As we retain a **high view of Scripture** and deepen our involvement in society while embodying a gospel that is relevant to our times, we will find ourselves with much more in common with some liberals we might otherwise have shunned. It is not unlike the sudden discovery by evangelicals touched by renewal in the 1970s that the Holy Spirit suddenly worked through the lives of [Roman] Catholics. There are liberals with a high view of Scripture, [and] a focus on Christ and the cross, whom we will be delighted to find as partners in the work of the gospel. Surely something to be celebrated!

• Aaron Fehir: **Evangelical-postmodern tensions**

First, I want to commend you on your project. I am deeply sympathetic and it is encouraging to see a group of Christian scholars engage in thoughtful discussion of "postmodernism." But the problem that you raise, i.e., how to define a postmodern evangelical, is one that I want here to complicate further.

First of all, there is a certain tension between postmodernism and evangelicalism. The former tends to be metaphysically antirealist and thus antithetical to **classical theism** (and I am thinking here of some of postmodernism's Christian authors—Caputo and Peperzak, for example). But it seems to me that a Christian couldn't rightly be considered evangelical unless she has a metaphysical conception of God as well as certain beliefs in, say, the **infallibility of Scripture** or the resurrection of Christ in history. So I wonder whether

Classical theism refers to the traditional approach to theology (inherited from ancient and medieval Christianity), which begins by defining God's attributes in terms of his being (as all-powerful, all-knowing, and all-good).

The "infallibility of Scripture" is closely related to the doctrine of inerrancy and emphasizes Scripture's authority in its pronouncements to compel belief.

the word "postmodern" which prefixes "evangelical" here is not actually a watered-down version of the real thing. It seems that a better word might be "**post-Cartesian**" or "**postfoundationalism**," and even there some difficulties would remain.

But this leads me to a second question. What of evangelical thinkers who stand in the tradition of **critical theory**? I can't think of anyone off the top of my head, but it would seem odd to me to call an evangelical **Habermasian** a postmodernist given Habermas' own critical stance toward the postmodernism of Gadamer, Foucault, and Derrida (who are three quite different thinkers).

Finally, there are many believers who affirm Christianity as it has been expressed in and through the creeds of the church and who affirm all the dogmas of traditional Christianity whom "postmodern evangelicals" share a great deal with, but who would be quite reluctant to take up one or the other (or both) of these titles: among them are conservative [Roman] Catholics and Eastern Orthodox, Reformationals [*sic*]/**Dooyeweerdians**, **Reformed epistemologists**, etc.

I just wonder if we ought not to be more blunt and make the division between left-leaning and right-leaning evangelicals.

Post-Cartesian simply means "coming after French philosopher René Descartes (seventeenth century)." Here it has more the meaning of "following the ideas of Descartes."

Postfoundationalism is treated in Bruce Benson's blog (Blog 3), but it simply refers here to a theory of knowledge that acknowledges there are no absolutely justified beliefs.

Critical theory is a twentieth-century philosophical movement (with roots back to Immanuel Kant) that, while critical of aspects of modernity, continues the Enlightenment task of freeing humans from forms of domination through rational critique—especially critique of social structures.

Jürgen Habermas is a contemporary German philosopher who deals with questions of critical theory, modernity, and postmodernity.

Herman Dooyeweerd (died 1977) was a Dutch Calvinist philosopher known especially for his belief that all philosophy and human thought makes religious assumptions.

Reformed epistemology argues that certain beliefs, like belief in God's existence, are properly called knowledge without any evidence to support them.

- Myron Bradley Penner: **Labels as useful fictions**

Aaron, thanks for your thoughtful post. I continue to think this is a useful discussion to have—the one about "postmodern evangelicalism"—even while I basically agree with you that there is a fuzziness about the terms and they eventually run out of usefulness. Such labels are, as I've stated elsewhere, "useful fictions" (see my "Christianity and the Postmodern Turn: Some Preliminary Considerations," in *Christianity and the Postmodern Turn: Six Views*, ed. Myron B. Penner [Grand Rapids: Brazos, 2003]); they enable us to become aware of a phenomenon, discuss and analyze it, but ultimately they break down. The trouble I have with your "left-leaning" and "right-leaning" labels is that they seem to me to be so fraught with baggage (conceptual and emotional, theological and political) that they will only divide us and obfuscate the issues.

And I think we're seeing evidence of the usefulness—and maybe even necessity—of the "postmodern evangelical" label here in this discussion. People are genuinely engaging what it means to be evangelical and modern or postmodern at the same time. I think that's helpful. For now. Perhaps we'll move past this discussion (and some, I know, hope we move past it soon!).

- Kenzo: **Knowledge, doubt, and evangelical faith**

I wholeheartedly agree with Myron, even in the ambiguity of his posting! One of the problems with Western theology, notwithstanding its major contribution to Christian theology, is that many of its advocates have an allergy for faith-based claims. Greek epistemology, especially Aristotelian epistemology, distinguishes at least three types of knowledge: knowledge of opinion (*opinio*), knowledge of faith (*fides*), and scientific knowledge (*scientia*). Without oversimplifying the historical development of theology, one may say that while the tradition that the church inherited from Augustine was more comfortable referring to theology as "wisdom" (*sapientia*) rather than science (*scientia*), medieval scholastics, seeking to justify the role of theology among the scientific disciplines of the then emerging universities, were set on seeing theology as a science. In so doing, they were willing to judge theology according to scientific criteria developed by Aristotle. According to Aristotle, scientific knowledge is (1) knowledge of essences, (2) knowledge according to causality, (3) knowledge of the necessary (over against the contingent), and (4) knowledge of the universal.

This tendency to define theology as a science according to secular criteria continued throughout the modern era, where it became radicalized. Whoever has any doubt can just read the introduction to Charles Hodge's *Systematic Theology*.[1] Hodge, who is no straw man, believed that theology is carried out with the same scientific rigor as physics. I believe J. I. Packer is correct to invite evangelical theologians to move past giants such as B. B. Warfield. The Warfields and the Hodges served their generation well; we have to do the same with ours (see "J. I. Packer, "Is Systematic Theology a Mirage?" in *Doing Theology in Today's World*, ed. John Woodbridge and Thomas McComiskey [Grand Rapids: Zondervan, 1991]). The postmodern critique of modernity has this virtue of reminding evangelicals that there is another tradition within Christian theology, which sought to preserve the uniqueness of Christian theology as faith seeking understanding. "O Lord, I do not seek to understand so that I may believe, but I seek to understand because I believe." So went St. Anselm's prayer. It does not take a genius to realize that Descartes' criteria for knowledge—that is, doubt-free clear and distinct ideas—is unattainable. As postmodern criticism sheds light on the hubris of the **Cartesian** pursuit, which, it needs to be said, was a highly contextual pursuit, it would be sad

Again, *Cartesian* simply refers to Descartes.

to claim for the truths of Christian faith the same characteristics that the former student from the College La Fleche claimed to have derived from unaided reason. Against Descartes, absolute epistemic certainty is not part of Christian faith. Doubt is always part of Christian experience. At times, the appropriate response to doubt is not more epistemic evidence, but more faith. "I do believe! O Lord, help my unbelief!"

THEOLOGY AND
(NON)(POST)FOUNDATIONALISM

Bruce Ellis Benson

Classical foundationalism is the belief that one's entire set of **epistemic commitments** can be grounded with absolute certainty by basic beliefs or arguments that, once given, would (at least theoretically) end all further discussion. For René Descartes, the philosopher most closely associated with modernism and foundationalism, the basic belief was "I think, therefore I am." On the basis of that one proposition, he was able to erect an entire system. With the rigorous expectations of **foundationalism** in place, modern theologians responded to their **naturalistic** counterparts with equally vigorous systems. Whereas theological liberals often found their bedrock in religious experience, conservatives often used the inerrant Scriptures as their foundation. Both of these moves were profoundly modern attempts to beat secular moderns at their own game.

Epistemic commitments refers to the beliefs we believe we know.

Foundationalism refers to theories of knowledge that describe human knowledge as built on certain foundational (or "basic") beliefs that themselves do not require evidence to warrant their belief—they're just knowledge.

Recall that *naturalism* is the worldview that says matter is all that there is. So the reference here is to secular atheists.

Yet classic foundationalism of modernity and its claims of **apodictic** certainty have recently fallen on hard times, for a number of reasons. Claims of a "universal objective reason" are increasingly questioned; the possibility of finding an **indubitable** starting point(s) seems unlikely to many; and even the idea that a self-evident belief could ground such a system has been shown to have itself been ungrounded. One need only think of the logical positivists, whose basic rule that propositions only be accepted as true if **empirically** or **analytically** demonstrated turned out not to pass its own test. As a result, some philosophers and theologians have moved to a "modest" or "soft" foundationalism, admitting that, while their foundations are not certain, they are still backed by reasonable evidence. But many others have rejected foundationalism as simply an unworkable project with unreasonable expectations.

> Recall that *apodictic* means something that can be clearly shown to be true.
>
> *Indubitable* refers to a belief that cannot possibly be doubted.
>
> *Empirical* refers to the experience of our five senses: what we see, hear, touch, taste, or smell.
>
> *Analytic* here refers to logical demonstration (as opposed to empirical sense experience).
>
> *Platonism* refers to the philosophy of the great ancient Greek philosopher Plato.
>
> *Empiricism* is the belief that all knowledge comes through the five senses.

Any postfoundational theology that hopes to go beyond modern foundationalism begins with at least one principal recognition: that beliefs about God and our relation to God are ultimately based on *faith*, with the insistence that it is *reasonable* to have such faith. This immediately raises the difficult question of the relation of faith and reason, one all the more complicated with the demise of foundationalism. The usual answer takes it cue from **Platonism**: knowledge is true belief (or faith) that is "grounded" (or, to use the typical contemporary phrase, knowledge is "justified true belief"). Yet, if the very notion of "grounding" is put in question (and, with it, what counts as "justified"), then suddenly that distinction seems considerably less clear-cut. While we might still use the term "knowledge" for things that have a high degree of evidence, there is a sense in which faith is not so far from knowledge. One might put that more pointedly by saying that knowledge presumes faith, in the sense that one's basic beliefs end up being taken on faith. If, for example, I am an **empiricist** and think that my basic beliefs come by way of the senses, then I am forced to assume my sensory perception is (at least most of the time) accurate. There is no way to provide a "foundation" for that belief. Postfoundationalists recognize that this is simply the way human understanding operates: it cannot ground itself. Moreover, rather than assume that there is something like "objective reason" with which all people will naturally agree, postfoundationalists assume instead that *all* respective starting points of theological or philosophical belief systems can *always* be questioned by others. Yet, with that recognition in mind, Christian postfoundationalists maintain that their basic beliefs—regarding God and the **veracity** of Scripture—are no less "plausible" than secular beliefs, and that one can hold them to be *true*. Even if they cannot be truly "justified" (in the modern sense of justification), one may still give reasons for holding them, all the while realizing that at a certain point one runs out of reasons.

Postfoundational theologians also recognize that our relation to God and the Bible is culturally conditioned. What is sometimes called "the hermeneutical turn" is the awareness that we always interpret doctrine and Scripture in light of our own situation. While some might see being culturally situated as a hindrance to true knowledge, postfoundationalists recognize that situatedness is actually a possibility condition *for* knowledge, and therefore not something to lament. To say that we know by way of what Gadamer calls "prejudices" is to say that our knowledge is never truly "objective."

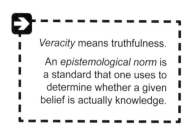

Veracity means truthfulness.

An *epistemological norm* is a standard that one uses to determine whether a given belief is actually knowledge.

While there are always differing degrees of objectivity, objectivity in the sense of being a "neutral, detached observer" is neither possible nor desirable. Even the apostle Paul notes that, to the Greeks, the good news seems like foolishness. So there is already the recognition in Scripture that where one is situated has important implications for the possibility of genuine understanding.

Further, postfoundationalists recognize that the modern category of "objectivity" is falsely attached to God, who is far from being a neutral, detached observer. Instead of relating to the world "objectively," God loves the world and hates sin. Thus, the so-called "God's eye view" is one that is itself *not* objective, even though it is the **epistemological norm**. Postfoundationalists insist that God's perspective on the world is what is presented to us in Scripture and it is that perspective that we should attempt—to the extent it is humanly possible—to make our own. Although some postfoundationalists would jettison **the correspondence theory of truth**, such a move is hardly entailed by being postfoundational. We may still believe that "true" is equivalent to "the way things are," but recognize that our knowledge of "the way things are" is (due to both **finitude** and sin) limited. Yet that does not mean that a genuine and true understanding of the world is not possible.

Even though the goal of having the mind of Christ is central to a postfoundationalist theology, postfoundationalists are particularly attuned to the dangers of "conceptual idolatry." They realize that it is all too easy to assume that our conceptions regarding God are exactly equivalent to who God truly is. Instead, they realize that human conceptions are always imperfect and inadequate (in the sense of a one-to-one **adequation**). Our ideas of God are always imperfect, and frequently marred by sin. Yet they likewise strenuously maintain that God's revelation to us is sufficient for human beings to truly know God, to have a personal relationship with God, and to be able to speak of God in meaningful and true ways. Postfoundationalists are likewise vigilant regarding interpretation of Scripture, always aware of the human tendency to interpret Scripture in ways that provide a rationale for human sinfulness.

Finally, postfoundational theologians take Scripture as their highest authority. It is the ultimate norm. Yet they likewise recognize that Scripture is not self-interpreting. **Sola scriptura** is taken to be the denunciation of the **Roman Catholic magisterium** as the true interpreter of Scripture, but not the denunciation of tradition as having an important effect upon interpretation. Indeed, postfoundationalists insist that Scripture must always be interpreted within a faith community and with the tradition of historic orthodoxy

The "correspondence theory of truth" is the traditional commonsense theory of truth which says that a belief or sentence is true when it corresponds to, or accurately reflects, the way reality really is.

Finitude refers to human limits.

Adequation means correspondence.

Sola scriptura literally means "Scripture alone," and was one of the central tenets of the Protestant Reformation.

Roman Catholic magisterium is a reference to the Roman Catholic belief that church tradition (i.e., the pope and the bishops in communion with him) authoritatively and infallibly interprets the truths of the faith.

as a guide. The recognition that right interpretation does not simply "happen" requires a strong reliance upon the Holy Spirit, the accountability of other believers as fellow interpreters, and a commitment to the idea that practical application of scriptural truth is a crucial part of the very interpretational process. Moreover, the goal of interpretation is always to make Scripture speak to the culture in which one is interpreting. Postfoundationalists realize that they walk a fine line between making Scripture relevant and accessible to the current culture while avoiding being co-opted by that culture. That requires both being part of culture while being able to maintain a critical stance regarding it.

COMMENTS

THREAD ONE:
Understanding Foundationalism

• David Schultz: **Foundationalism and straw men**

For theologians who keep setting up **straw men** about foundationalism, or "classical foundationalism," we need to get past that. "Modest foundationalism" has made its place in philosophical circles because of writers like Robert Audi (*Epistemology: A Contemporary Introduction*).[1] Knowledge, all philosophers understand, doesn't require certainty (it's not part of any **tripartite analysis** or any other analysis of knowing), and they have known it for one hundred or more years; there are some kinds of knowledge that possess certainty (a priori). But because modest foundationalism dispenses (or at least "postfoundationalists" do) with certainty for basic beliefs and deductive inference from them, it does not follow that they are based on faith: it's not either/or—certainty or faith. When Benson asserts without argument, "There is no way to provide a 'foundation' for that [basic] belief," he's just uninformed, philosophically, of the vast literature on the subject. Of course there is a way to do it; just read some philosophers who have thought about it.

I see a huge problem, which this is a symptom of (and at the schools I teach at): that classically trained, professional philosophers like me talk

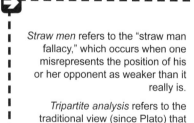

Straw men refers to the "straw man fallacy," which occurs when one misrepresents the position of his or her opponent as weaker than it really is.

Tripartite analysis refers to the traditional view (since Plato) that knowledge has three parts: a) justified; b) true; c) belief.

past evangelical theologians (I see it in **JETS** and in **Grenz/Franke**, everywhere) because, frankly, theologians have set up straw men about foundationalism, and philosophers are too busy to redebate old ground. I think we need an open and honest dialogue between them—theologians and philosophers—and keep it civil, but let's not make bald claims based on misinformed opinions. Leave the philosophy to the philosophers; then talk to us so that we all get it right; and we'll come to you for theological points when we need to. But uninformed theologians making uninformed arguments isn't moving us forward. No one will take us seriously. At the Catholic university I teach at there are theologians who are as good at philosophy as I am (!!); I don't see that often in evangelicalism. We need to stop getting mad and calling each other names, and get serious and do our research, or we just won't be taken seriously—and that for right reasons.

> JETS = The *Journal of the Evangelical Theological Society*
>
> Stanley J. Grenz and John R. Franke wrote a book together entitled *Beyond Foundationalism: Shaping Theology in a Postmodern Context* (Louisville: Westminster John Knox, 2001).
>
> J. P. Moreland is presently a professor of philosophy at Talbot School of Theology at Biola University and is an outspoken critic of postmodernism.

We are creating a terminology that creates a vocabulary wherein we just talk among ourselves and past ourselves. The term "postfoundational" is one piece of a large puzzle that has been turned into a cornerstone. I am an evangelical postfoundationalist foundationalist (and premodernist), and those who refer to themselves as "we postfoundationalists" and still keep talking about basic beliefs not requiring faith are wonderfully simplistic. Agreed, philosophers within evangelicalism haven't always acted like adults here; but the frustration is that some of us see oversimplification, straw men, and uninformed opinion while we work hard on making fine distinctions about these things, and it's ignored. Therein lies the frustration and the reason for the kind of remarks **Moreland** has made at times.

- Chris Criminger: **Both/And**

This issue has become so polemical between foundationalists and nonfoundationalists, but I love David Schultz's response because his is truly a *both/and* approach to this issue, recognizing the truth within both sides of the debate rather than just accepting one side or viewing this issue in either/or terms—i.e., either one must be a foundationalist or a nonfoundationalist (which also gets translated by some as "antifoundationalist"). Thank you, David.

• Jonathan Wood: **Theology without foundations**

First of all, David, I don't think that anybody here is really "getting mad and calling each other names." I believe this may be a bit harsh. Furthermore, it seems to me that maybe you have missed the gist of Professor Benson's argument, namely that "beliefs about God and our relation to God are ultimately based on *faith*." Postfoundationalists (or rather those who adhere to the maxim above) are also post-modest-foundationalists. The claim being made by (many) postfoundationalists is that theology is not grounded in an epistemology; it is not contingent on philosophy for its categories, concepts, and ideas (although it may use them from time to time). Theology is grounded in faith, and although there may be at times good reasons for faith this does not necessarily imply that these are "logical" reasons. As **Pascal** says, "The heart has its reasons of which reason knows nothing."

> Blaise Pascal, an early-seventeenth-century French mathematician and philosopher, wrote a collection of thoughts, compiled together and published as *Pensées*.

[David, you commented on J. P. Moreland's remarks.] In this are you referring to such comments that he has made in the March 2005 *Journal of the Evangelical Theological Society*, that "postmodernism is an immoral and cowardly viewpoint"? This, if anything, seems to be an example of what you refer to as "calling each other names."

• Bruce Ellis Benson: **Clarifications**

To David Schultz: Good to hear from a "classically trained, professional philosopher" like yourself, and from a Catholic university to boot! My doctorate is from the Katholieke Universiteit Leuven (the oldest Catholic university in the world), where I was classically trained in both analytic and continental philosophy. I have to confess: I'm a philosopher, not a theologian. So maybe I shouldn't have been allowed to write this section on theology! By the way, I'm well acquainted with Robert Audi, a fine philosopher and someone whom I've met, as well as Alvin Plantinga. You mention Audi and, by inference, it sounds like you refer to Plantinga. You quote me as saying, "There is no way to provide a 'foundation' for that belief [in the validity of one's senses]." One can say that such a belief is **"properly basic"** or simply say that the foundation for belief in the senses can't be given. I happen to believe that it can't. However, that belief is not based on an ignorance of the literature, but on an acquaintance with it. Being acquainted with the literature, of course, is not the same as agreeing with it. Although I don't mention Audi, I do note (in paragraph two) that there are those who have "moved to a 'modest' or 'soft' foundationalism." So I am well aware that there are varieties of foundationalists out there.

To Chris Criminger: As to the term "foundationalist," I'm neither for or against it. I can well see why some would want to retain the terminology. You're right that, for some, postfoundationalism gets translated as "antifoundationalism" (by both supporters and detractors).

> *Properly basic* is a technical term in the theory of knowledge that refers to beliefs for which we have no evidence but are still knowledge.

To Jonathan Wood: Thanks for your clarification. It's right on target. I was saddened by those remarks from Moreland (which you quote) when I first heard them at the 2004 Evangelical Theological Society annual conference. Fortunately, Myron Penner has written a very fine paper in response to Prof. Moreland that strikes a proper tone for a discussion with a brother in Christ. [See Myron B. Penner, "Cartesian Anxiety, Perspectivalism and Truth: A Response to J. P. Moreland," *Philosophia Christi* 8/1 (Summer 2006): 85–98.]

- David Schultz: **Theology must have foundations!**

To Mr. Wood: [You mention doing theology without foundations or grounds.] Look to Hegel for an example, and possibly even [earlier to] later Plato for coherentist theologies. I would say we cannot do it. But **coherentism** has problems of its own, and we need to consider them before we jump on the bandwagon.

I hear much of doing away with foundations, but I don't have a clear idea from the literature what they will be replaced with. I think this is a crucial question for us all (but see below, too).

[You say,] "I don't think that anybody here is really 'getting mad and calling each other names.' I believe this may be a bit harsh." Have you read some of the journals? Have you been in the corners where scholars gather to talk among themselves? I do refer to Moreland and others. It's just unhelpful.

To Dr. Benson: [You mention that you are aware of the varieties of foundationalism.] I don't mean to call into question anyone's competency—that would fall into the trap I am arguing against. (I trained with Robert Audi, by the way, and still speak to him every so often.) I am sure you are aware of these [varieties]. But some [postfoundationalist theologians] reject foundationalism by pointing out that **Cartesian foundationalism** has fallen (which it has), and then immediately move to a nonfoundationalist stance, as if modest foundationalism doesn't exist. That is where someone like me looks at the argument and feels puzzled (in a **Pyrrhonist** sense!). The argument doesn't go through because

> Coherentism here refers to the theory that what justifies a given belief is the way it relates to (or "coheres with," logically sticks together with) other beliefs we have. In other words, coherentists say we are justified in believing something just so long as it doesn't conflict with something else we believe.
>
> *Cartesian foundationalism* refers to Descartes' theory of knowledge.
>
> Pyrrho of Elea was an ancient Greek skeptic who held that certainty in knowledge is not possible.
>
> *Contra* = "against"
>
> *Simpliciter* = "straightforwardly"; here it is used to mean something like "in its simple form."
>
> *Regress* here means that the justifying process keeps going on forever (so that in the end it cannot actually be justified). For example, belief x is justified by y, and y is justified by z, and z is justified by something else, and so on infinitely.

it's an argument **contra** one species of foundationalism as a stand-in for all species (because it is foundationalism **simpliciter** that is being argued against, not a species of it, I believe). To show [that] foundationalism itself (modest, strong, or any other variety), is false, one would have to show we *need* no foundations epistemically (for justification), and [that] this leads to no **regress**, and that coherentism isn't circular. In other words, [postfoundationalist theologians] have to respond to the basic argument for foundationalism, **the regress argument**. I haven't seen it.

Yet, if one argues thusly, one is put in the strange-sounding position that his [or her] theology/knowledge is not based on anything (a sort of **epistemic nihilism** leading to **fideism**?)—it is [supposed to be] based on *nothing*, yet I then hear it's based on faith. So which is it? What I am arguing is that you cannot escape the language [of foundationalism] because it reflects the deep structure of our thought and this is why Aristotle's regress argument (for example) is so remarkably long-lasting. I am not trying to **beg questions** here (and say that foundationalism is true just because that is the way the mind works). I am simply saying that the near necessity of having to speak about foundations should tell us something; even coherentists slip in some connection to the world/mind and so, as Audi would argue, are really closet foundationalists!

> The *regress argument* appealed to here simply states that if one has an infinite regress of justification (described above), one does not have knowledge. Put differently, the buck has to stop somewhere—and where it stops is a foundation upon which we build knowledge!
>
> Again, *epistemic nihilism* is the denial of the possibility of knowledge.
>
> *Fideism* is the view that says faith does not need to have reasons to justify it.
>
> *Begging the question* is a logical fallacy that occurs when someone attempts to prove a point by using an argument that assumes the truth of the very conclusion for which they are arguing. Example: "How do you know the Bible is true?" Answer— "The Bible says so."
>
> *Disjunction* happens when two terms are placed together and one or the other may be true, but not both; they are separated by an "or."

So, [would] some postfoundationalist please clarify [for me] what [it] means to say, "My theology is based on *nothing*" (which a postfoundationalist would have to accept)? Because if [one's theology] is based on faith it's based on something rather than nothing and no longer postfoundational. Nancy Murphy says that our theology is based on *either* the Bible or experience. Though she notes in a footnote that this is a simplification, I wonder why only in a footnote! [Editors' note: We're not sure where in Nancy Murphy's work David is referring.]

My second argument [against postfoundational theology] would be along the lines of pointing out that the **disjunction** "faith or foundationalism" is false and incomplete. First, there are foundationalists who have no faith, and there are post-foundationalists who say they do. Why can't we be people of faith who happen to be foundationalists as well? The **white noise** I hear in the background of many discussions is that if we base faith on anything other than itself or Scripture we somehow lose something spiritually important. But theology from the bottom up has to start someplace, and this doesn't rob my theology of any spiritual substance or make it more open to attacks because I've left the **eristic** refuge of fideism.

[You mentioned that you were saddened by J. P. Moreland's comments, and that Myron has written a good response to him. I was actually trying to say that] we don't need [Moreland's] kind of [response]. However, I understand his frustration *as a philosopher*. It's time we sit at the same table and hammer this stuff out if we are to be taken seriously by those outside our academic community. People are watching us.

I guess what troubles me the most is this: I see us as trying escape the snares of modernism that have crept into our theology by embracing postmodernism. One hundred years from now we'll be trying to escape the snares of the post-modernism that we welcomed into our faith today (the way early modernist Christians did with modernism). I my-self think we do need a tradition to assist theology, so I understand the search. I

> *White noise* refers to background noise; in this context it is used to refer to the ideas behind what people are saying.
>
> *Eristic* refers to a debater's strategy of arguing to win a debate, as opposed to getting at the truth.
>
> In this case, *Classical Tradition* probably means the tradition of rational inquiry that is characteristic of Western philosophy, beginning with the ancient Greek philosophers, along with the Christian theological tradition that merged with philosophy during the medieval era.
>
> *Patristics* refers to the "church fathers," or the Christian thinkers of the first four or five centuries.
>
> *Telos* is a Greek word meaning "end, purpose, or goal."

also think that the **Classical Tradition** [*sic*] serves us well (not just the **patristics**, though that gives a model of how the Classical Tradition was used). In fact, most of the "good things" that evangelicals (I am one, by the way) claim we need to appropriate from postmodernism have antecedents in the Classical Tradition (Aristotle and community, for example), I would argue.

Cheers! I think the spirit [in this discussion] is really very good and helpful. Let's air out these things and remain committed to the same **telos**—Christ.

- Jonathan Wood: **Existential-pragmatic foundations for faith**

David: Good points of clarification. I must say that after everyone has posted their resumes I feel greatly incompetent (I may be the only one here who hasn't studied with Robert Audi [insert laugh here]). Nonetheless, despite incompetence I will keep on talking, like I always do (insert second laugh here).

In response to your statement [about postfoundational faith needing to be based on something:] I agree. I guess the real question of conversation lies in agreeing what this "something" is that faith is based on. The whole significance of the "post" in postfoundationalism, as I understand it, is not akin to antifoundationalism or nonfoundationalism, but merely a mark of the conscious decision to shift foundations within theology.

As I see it, theology is not based on nothing; it is based on paradox. Such fundamental, central doctrines to Christian faith as **the hypostatic union of Christ's two natures** (man/God, finite/infinite), the Trinity (three = one), and "He who wishes to save his life must lose it" all demarcate an impasse to reason. Not only are these central doctrines impassable to reason/logic, they are actually an offense to reason/logic (all of them defy the most basic rule of logic, **Aristotle's law of noncontradiction**). How does reason understand that Christ was fully God and fully human? It doesn't. How does reason understand that God is both one and three? It doesn't. How does reason understand that it must kill itself if it wants to live? It doesn't. It is the passion of faith alone that drives the individual to cross the logical impasse. This is also the same passion that, afterward, causes the individual to reorient what he or she thinks is reason and understanding.

> ➡ *Hypostatic union* refers to the classic doctrine of Christ's two natures, affirmed at the council of Chalcedon in 451 AD, according to which Jesus was both fully human and fully divine, two natures in one person, without any mixture of the natures.
>
> *Aristotle's law of noncontradiction* states that "A is not non-A"; or, a thing cannot be both what it is and is not.

This is the "reason" why I think faith is qualitatively different than the kind of foundationalism proposed by classical foundationalists and modest foundationalists (as well as some coherentists who were not so opposed to paradoxes, like Hegel), essentially because it is not necessarily "epistemic" along these terms.

Yes, of course there are reasons for faith; however, I understand these as **existential reasons** rather than logical reasons—for instance, the despair of trying to live life with oneself as one's ultimate authority.

For this reason, if somebody asks me why [he or she] should become a Christian, (because of my postfoundation approach to theology) I don't say, "Because it makes sense"—I say, "Because it has infinitely more to offer you than any other way of living your life. However, beware . . . it will cost you your life."

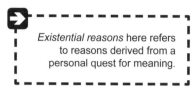

Existential reasons here refers to reasons derived from a personal quest for meaning.

- David Schultz: **Postfoundationalist = Post-certitude?**

BTW: My move in saying [that a postfoundationalist's theology is] "based on nothing" is typical of an analytic philosopher like myself; I don't mean it as a slight but as a philosophical point about language use; that is, if we reject foundationalism we are in the strange position of having to say such and such. Again, it's a classical move in the philosophical language-game (the whole post was basically a polemical move trying to express what we philosophers think when we hear others talk).

[Your point that] "the real question of conversation lies in agreeing what this 'something' is that faith is based on" [and that] "the whole significance of the 'post' in postfoundationalism" [has to do with a] "conscious decision to shift foundations within theology" is the most helpful thing anyone has said so far (for my dense brain anyway). Now I think we're making progress! If the debate is about changing foundations, then we have something to talk about!

If, in fact, there are five sources (foundations) for knowing (perception, memory, reason, introspection, and let's throw in testimony), then when someone says that theology is "based on Scripture," she or he means "based on testimony." Now as historical and contingent, theology lacks certainty, not because the Cartesian edifice has crumbled but simply because the nature of the foundation requires it. . . . If by "postfoundational" one means, as you suggest, the rejection of certainty, then I am on board! Why not say it's a "post-certitude" stance?

Oh—and one thing I find interesting: I think people are confusing "postmodernism" with "postmodernity" (a distinction made in the literature). Certainly we live in postmodernity (a late-capitalist, global, postindustrial, and so on world), but we're not all postmodernists in that we accept postmodernism. I see people trying to make the distinction, and one can find it in Kellner and Best's books on postmodernism,[2] for example.

- Bruce Ellis Benson: **Foundationalism, faith, and "straw men"**

To David Schultz: First, thanks for your email. I completely agree with you that, once someone moves away from foundations, it often becomes unclear what is replacing them. Further, I agree that an argument against Descartes isn't an argument against all foundationalism. However, on my read, modest foundationalism sounds contradictory. Foundationalism is all about grounding, which from my perspective is all about certainty. Maybe I just misread the project, but from what you say in a later post it sounds like we agree. The idea that there are basic beliefs that need no justification sounds like a version of faith, not foundationalism, to me. But I'm with you on the dangers of "escaping" modernism only to be ensnared by postmodernism. I think we have to be careful of both. By the way, in regard to your later post in which you talk about the difference between "postmodernity" and "postmodernism," I think that's a helpful distinction to make. But then we're still left with what we mean by "postmodernism," and there's no clear consensus on that.

To Jonathan Wood: I agree that the "foundation" is theological and that it's also based on paradoxes. But once you make that move, then the whole notion of foundation changes (as David astutely notes).

[Editors' note: David Schultz replied that he found Bruce's position on modest foundationalism to be a straw man argument.]

. . . To David Schultz: Thanks very much for your comments. I appreciate being pushed to think harder on this issue.

If I've created a straw man by saying that "modest foundationalism sounds contradictory," that certainly wasn't my intent. I wasn't thinking of Descartes per se, just of the "foundationalist" project as I understand it. To be honest, I simply don't see your point (the implied point that I'm "stuck in a modernist paradigm"). I have no problem with the project of modest foundationalism, just its name. But if you're happy with the name, that's fine with me.

As to your comment [that I seem to think that all foundationalists are idealists], that could not have been further from my mind. You said, "Most foundationalists I know are not idealists," which must mean that you know at least one who is. I don't know any (except **Husserl**, whom I never met).

I don't mean at all to suggest that "because belief stops" "it does so arbitrarily." [Editors' note: David Schultz wrote, "Because belief stops, it doesn't follow that it does so arbitrarily. A foundation is simply where **justificatorial** demands end."] I completely understand the idea of a "foundation" being a belief at which "justificatorical demands end." I just don't agree with the idea that such a belief provides a "foundation." There may be evidence—even very good evidence—for that belief, but I balk at the notion of calling it a "foundation." Here I think the terminology gets in the way. I understand how you're using the term, but I don't use it that way myself. I should say that I find your idea of beliefs "floating" to be quite compelling. You say you hold such a conception because you "see the foundationalist structure as more fluid than some." Again, [I am in] complete agreement. But, then, the view you're putting forth sounds even less like "foundationalism" to me.

> Edmund Husserl was an early-twentieth-century German philosopher widely known as the father of phenomenology—an approach to philosophy that focuses on the way we consciously experience the world.
>
> *Justification* is a category in the theory of knowledge that refers to the reasons that are used to support a belief in such a way that it is actually knowledge, and not just mere opinion. The end of justificatorial demands, mentioned here, simply refers to a situation in which we can no longer give reasons for belief. One example might be our beliefs that we are alive.
>
> *Fideistically* = without regard for reason

When I say that "foundationalism is all about grounding, which from my perspective is all about certainty," I'm simply going by the literature on the subject. Are there philosophers out there who don't think that strong foundationalism is about certainty?

My use of the term "faith" does not denote something that one holds **fideistically**, so it does not entail "no justification." Rather, its justification is limited: a kind of justification that does not lead to rational certainty (even if it might lead to a kind of existential certainty, as in the case of Pascal). But it is not without grounds (and I have no problem using those terms).

THREAD TWO:
BIBLICAL INTERPRETATION, REASON, AND TRUTH

- Jeff: **Biblical authority and self-interpretation**

If Scripture is the "highest authority" and the "ultimate norm" [as Bruce says,] how is it even remotely possible that it isn't supposed to interpret itself? What authority is left to do the interpreting: a lower authority? Who will then be the final arbiter of disputes?

- Bruce Ellis Benson: **Scripture does not interpret itself!**

Jeff, if you can give me an example of a book interpreting itself, I'd be most obliged. I've never seen that happen before. Instead, books are interpreted by people interpreting them. There are, as far as I can tell, no self-interpreting musical scores either. To be interpreted, someone has to play them. You ask, "Who will then be the final arbiter of disputes?" Well, the answer to that depends on which Christian tradition you are a part of. If you're a Roman Catholic, then it's the **magisterium**. If you're a Protestant of some sort or another, then there isn't an immediate "final arbiter" (unless you attend a very fundamentalist, independent

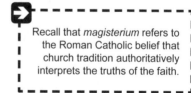

Recall that *magisterium* refers to the Roman Catholic belief that church tradition authoritatively interprets the truths of the faith.

church, in which case it's the pastor). Note that this problem doesn't go away if we say that the Bible interprets itself. Even evangelicals who think the Bible interprets itself disagree regarding particular passages in Scripture. Just read the commentaries of evangelicals and that becomes clear.

- Jeff: **Two examples of Scripture interpreting itself**

I'm a little stunned by your challenge. Unless I misunderstood the term "self-interpreting," there are too many instances in Scripture where it would seem to interpret itself. . . . Let me just give two: 1) John 5:39: This is easily the Lord

Jesus telling the Jews what the ultimate meaning and purpose of Scripture was. 2) Ephesians 4:8–9: This is just one example of two possible ways the New Testament interprets the rest of Scripture—first, by quoting it; second, by explaining what it meant in precise terms.

But my original rhetorical question had to do with the inconsistency of saying something is an ultimate authority, then devising a secondary system or tradition that can override the meaning. What happens when the secondary system or tradition contradicts or adds to the previously determined authority? Who decides which is right? The answer is no one. Who can? Only God can say what he meant with any authority. Then he does teach those willing to listen. So he becomes the last, great "ultimate authority." That is what is important to remember.

I have trouble with tradition as an authority on anything, even with my shallow knowledge of church history. Tradition might teach us what *not* to do. Yes, the commentaries highlight man's failure, too.

- Bruce Ellis Benson: **Tradition is essential for biblical interpretation**

To Jeff: The first example you provide is of Jesus interpreting the Scripture. In other words, it's an act of interpretation. The second example is that of Paul doing the interpreting. Yes, their interpretations are now part of Scripture. But even when we read their interpretations, we still have to interpret them ourselves. Further, you've provided two instances of one part of Scripture interpreting another part. While that's not uncommon in Scripture, it's certainly not the norm.

I well understand your point of the problem of me saying that Scripture is an ultimate authority and then turning around and talking about something else. Tradition would be part of it, so Scripture has to be read in the context of the church and its history. But so would having a command of language. You may have "trouble with tradition as an authority on anything," but I don't see how interpretation is possible without these **ancillary** things (tradition, language, etc.).

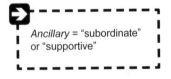

Ancillary = "subordinate" or "supportive"

That does not mean that tradition is "over and above" Scripture; it just means that tradition is a [necessary] supplement [to it].

- Whitewave: **God, not Scripture, is the highest authority**

I see Jeff's point here. This is why I can no longer include myself within the realm of "evangelicals." I just don't feel obligated anymore to find a roundabout way to agree that Scripture is the "highest authority." I've left that whole thing behind.

I agree that God is the highest authority. And from there he has expressed and manifested himself in four main ways: 1) Jesus Christ; 2) "the Scriptures" (which interpret themselves sometimes, and at other times deny their own "Scripturehood"—e.g., 1 Corinthians 7:12); 3) the Holy Spirit present within the people of God right now; and 4) tradition—which is the Holy Spirit present within the people of God, gently and gradually unfolding a truth that is often too large for our small humanness, through time. I keep those last two separate for the purposes of keeping the wineskin fresh enough to contain God's next move.

It's pretty clear that people interpret the Scripture. People's interpretations of Scripture have become considered Scripture, even when a writer is clearly claiming something different than Scripture for the status of his writing. Christians do that. At least the Jewish people have different names for all these distinctions—bless them.

I don't know. I just don't think it's necessary anymore to hold on to that evangelical bit about the Scripture being the highest authority. Especially since (for evangelicals, not Luther) the intent is to universalize and bring about unity by agreement, but it has totally failed at this. I think it's important now to refresh the intent, but let the failed methods drop away.

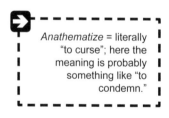

Anathematize = literally "to curse"; here the meaning is probably something like "to condemn."

I really like what the Orthodox contribute to this, though they have also failed in some important ways. Is there a way to integrate all these methods which more or less have the same intent—i.e., to protect the truth that God has given us from being co-opted and corrupted by limited human beings—and have them all check one another without **anathematizing** one another?

- Matthew M. Thomas: **Truth is a person**

In our discussions of epistemology, we seem to focus primarily on the locus of truth. It seems that both foundationalists and postfoundationalists do this. It seems that we are asking, "Is truth something that can be made an 'object' in the sense that it can be examined from the outside, apprehended, analyzed, and [tested in a laboratory]; or is truth something that is so inseparable from our experience, language, and culture that such experiments cannot be run accurately and provide us with useful knowledge; or is it something in between?"

Both of these viewpoints tend to maintain the notion that truth is an object per se, but that its locus causes it to be more or less knowable due to the ability (or lack thereof) to disentangle it from our own experience. There is, even in postfoundationalism, a hint that truth is something that can be written down and codified—and "Oh, wouldn't it be nice if we could disentangle it from experience/culture/language, but we can't."

However, assuming a postfoundationalist viewpoint allows us to dig into epistemology a little deeper to bring a theological perspective to bear on the discussion of truth. In doing so, we move the epistemological dialogue from the locus of truth to its nature. Theologically, we accept (to varying degrees) the idea that the truth is a person. Affirming faith in one who claims to be *the* truth—one who is both fully divine and fully human—we discover that the way we perceive that we must access truth must undergo transformation.

If truth is an object—however much it may be entangled or disentangled with our experience—we come to know that truth in a particular way granted to objects. If, however, truth is a person, we come to know that truth in a different way. Terms such as "objective" and "absolute" make a lot less sense. More importantly, "understanding" takes on different meaning. "Understanding" a person is very different than "understanding" a concept or an object.

If truth is a person, then truth that is entangled in culture, language, personality, perspective, and experience is not only permissible but can be seen to be the primary way in which its content may be apprehended. Furthermore, the question of "content" is less urgent, as we realize the discernment of the "content" of a person makes little sense to us.

The epistemology of truth as a person is, in some sense, nonfoundationalist or postfoundationalist, in that it does not attempt to work propositionally from the **first principle** to all others. It assumes, via faith, that getting to know this particular person, Jesus Christ, will open us to a greater understanding of that which is true. This further implies that we interact with truth relationally, rather than abstractly. Because truth is relational, we cannot go

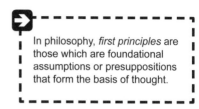

In philosophy, *first principles* are those which are foundational assumptions or presuppositions that form the basis of thought.

back to the first principle, because to do so we would have to disassociate ourselves relationally from truth and thus have no way to relate to it once we got back to the first principle (if we could even get back that far, having disengaged from our relational interactions with truth).

In some ways, "truth is a person" becomes a kind of first principle. Nevertheless, it is not a first principle after the manner of *cogito ergo sum* (I think, therefore I am). It cannot be examined externally. However, it is this sort of status that gives the theological permission we need to recognize our cultural conditioning.

For if truth is a person, the person of Jesus Christ, then truth is inseparable from a first-century Palestinian Jew, who on the day of Pentecost began to relate to widely diverse cultures across time and place to bring complete salvation to the whole world.

• Bruce Ellis Benson: **Limits of "objectivity"**

Matthew: You make an excellent point in distinguishing between truth as an object and a person. Jesus says, "I am the way, and the truth, and the life" (John 14:6 NASB). Unless we take that as merely a metaphorical statement, then Jesus is truth. You're right that in such a case "objective" and "absolute" make a lot less sense. But let me take that a little further by saying that "objective" (at least) doesn't make a great deal of sense in much of the way in which we know the "truth" of Scripture. Being a believer is not very accurately described in "objective" terms.

THE BIBLE, THEOLOGY, AND POSTMODERNISM

Myron Bradley Penner

However else we evangelicals have identified ourselves in North America, the doctrine of Scripture lies at the core of our identity and self-understanding. Over and against modern liberal theologians who accepted the dictates of higher criticism in regard to the Christian Scriptures, evangelicals stood in the gap, refused to bend to modern attacks on the Bible, and developed an elaborate apologetic **bibliology** that asserted the full authority of Scripture and its propositional inerrancy. Couple this with the fact that many (most?) evangelicals perceive postmodernism as seriously compromising the ability of the biblical (or any other) text to say anything meaningful at all and it is understandable why a large contingent of evangelicals react very negatively to the encroachment of postmodernism on Christian thought. Those of us who identify with evangelicalism but are also com-

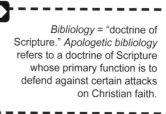

Bibliology = "doctrine of Scripture." *Apologetic bibliology* refers to a doctrine of Scripture whose primary function is to defend against certain attacks on Christian faith.

pelled by aspects of the postmodern turn need to be mindful of the historical value of the evangelical response to theological liberalism and how much our ability to be (self)critical of evangelicalism in a postmodern way owes to those early evangelicals. Nonetheless, it is my firm conviction that the traditional evangelical doctrine of Scripture[1] needs to be retooled in the light of postmodern critiques of the modern philosophical framework in which evangelicals have situated their view of the Bible. I want to offer several brief suggestions as to what such a "retooling" might look like.

First, a comment or two is in order regarding our general approach to Scripture and its relation to Jesus. An evangelical doctrine of Scripture needs to have the *evangel*, the gospel of Jesus Christ, at its center. Subsequently, evangelicals need to rearticulate their thinking about Scripture so that we move beyond a bibliology whose primary focus and value is the apologetic establishment of an authoritative epistemic basis for doctrine. Such thinking severely truncates the value of Scripture and is, in fact, at odds with the way Scripture speaks about itself. We evangelicals often have a difficult time dealing consistently with the claims in John's Gospel that Jesus is the *logos* and that *he* is the way, the truth, and the life. The point of the gospel (according to the four evangelists, St. Paul, and the rest of the New Testament) is not the Bible, but Jesus. (Compare Jesus' denunciation of such an attitude toward Scripture as recorded in John 5:39–40.)

We evangelicals often run perilously close to validating the charge from our Roman Catholic brothers and sisters who find the Protestant emphasis on Scripture a form of "**bibliolatry**." We need, in other words, a view of Scripture that captures and embodies the truth that "The Holy Scriptures are the highway signs: Christ is the way."[2]

> *Bibliolatry* is a term used to denote an idolatrous fixation on Scripture, worshiping it rather than God.
>
> *Epiphenomenon* = a secondary event related to another primary event

Thinking of Scripture in terms that combine Karl Barth's notion of God's "indirect identity" in and with his revelation[3] with the postmodern insight that language is a medium that provides the conditions for the possibility of human understanding would go a long ways toward establishing a perspective on Scripture in which the *evangel* was placed front and center. In this way we may come closer to seeing how the written text of Scripture is intimately and necessarily connected to Jesus as the *logos*, as a sort of **epiphenomenon** to God's primary revelation in Jesus' incarnation.

Second, I like Kevin Vanhoozer's suggestion that evangelicals should adopt a view of Scripture that is "postpropositional."[4] Scripture, by its own attestation

(2 Timothy 3:16–17) and through its use of multiple literary forms and genres, contains more than just **propositional revelation**. Thus, when we reduce the content of the biblical revelation to **propositions** we dangerously distort the text with modern philosophical assumptions about the nature of truth and meaning. The sort of postpropositional approach to Scripture I am calling for here is not one that denies that God speaks in Scripture in propositional form, but is an approach that acknowledges that God performs many different types of **speech acts** in Scripture and insists that conveying propositional truths is often not the primary point. There are a variety of **revelational media** referred to and employed in Scripture (cf. Hebrews 1:1–2). A postpropositional approach to Scripture places its confidence in Scripture because of its ability to "make us wise unto salvation," not because it is a storehouse of universal, infallible, true propositions. (This, in turn, suggests that evangelicals need to adjust their truth theories to accommodate the different ways in which Scripture is true.)

From a postpropositional perspective, then, the evangelical fixation on the doctrine of inerrancy and its corresponding **grammatical-historical method of interpretation** continues an infatuation with modern philosophical categories. The latter case is simply a capitulation to modern assumptions regarding the authority of universal and "objective" human reason in the interpretive process and regarding the determinateness of textual meaning. A postpropositional approach, as I construe it, assumes that God has spoken and *is speaking* in the text, that it is "living and active" (Hebrews 4:12), and that God may be performing a number of speech acts in any given passage, addressing a number of audiences. Digging into the grammatical and historical contexts of a

> *Propositional revelation* is revelation (the revealing of God's truth) in human language in the form of declarative sentences.
>
> Recall that *propositions* are basically declarative sentences.
>
> The term *speech act* is taken from a theory of language that views language as primarily about certain actions we perform by speaking (like giving an order, or asking a question, or making a promise), rather than the more traditional view that language is about connecting meanings of words together in a string in order to convey information.
>
> *Revelational media* here refers to different ways God reveals himself, like, for example, through Scripture, prophecy, nature, etc.
>
> The *grammatical-historical method of interpretation* views the grammatical and historical background of a passage as the key to its meaning.

passage is one (albeit important) aspect of the biblical text's meaning, but it is not exhaustive. Postmodern evangelicals should, then, look to Scripture in order to *open* debates, by setting the parameters and mode of address to theological issues, more than they look to it to *settle* debates.

I will restrain myself to just two more quick comments about the evangelical doctrine of inerrancy. First, as Vanhoozer has so ably pointed out, inerrancy is not a hermeneutic.[5] So even if the Bible *is* inerrant, it is possible we may never be able even to access the ways in which it is inerrant (i.e., obtain inerrant truths from it), let alone *prove* the Bible to be such. This in no way means that inerrancy is irrelevant to exegesis and just biblical interpretation in general, but it greatly reduces its relevance for the hermeneutic enterprise—and does so in a way that falsifies a great deal of what I suspect many evangelicals take to be the gist of the doctrine of inerrancy (i.e., to produce "absolute truths"). Second, inerrancy treats the text of Scripture as if the goals and intentions of its author(s) are the same as those of a modern theologian or philosopher. Modern philosophers **reified** propositional truth as the only form of truthful affirmation because propositions, as they conceived them, enjoy the luxury of being "objective," abstract, and universal. As defined in modernity, propositions (roughly) are whatever is expressed by a declarative sentence and therefore expresses what is open to public evaluation and is translatable into the declarative sentences of any natural language. When evangelicals fixate on inerrancy as an attempt to shore up the truthfulness and authority of Scripture, we do so because we explicitly or implicitly buy into these assumptions about truth and language and expect that Scripture itself assumes these things. However, as already referred to, 2 Timothy 3:16–17 describes Scripture as *useful* for a variety of purposes.

> *Reify* here means something like "to take an immaterial thing and treat it as if it were something material or real."

This point naturally leads to the issue of hermeneutics, which is the third area of an evangelical doctrine of Scripture I want to emphasize as needing revision in light of the postmodern critiques of modernity. A postmodern view of Scripture has no problem acknowledging that whatever is affirmed in Scripture is wholly and completely true. Insofar as inerrancy is an attempt to preserve the truthfulness of God and his speech, I applaud it and wholeheartedly agree with it. Inerrancy isn't *wrong*, so much as it is *wrong-headed*. The key issue, though, has to do with what Scripture, taken as a whole and in any given piece, is *actually affirming*. Postmodern questions about inerrancy concern, on the one hand, our access to these inerrant truths and, on the other hand, the form and content these truths take. In other words, postmodern evangelicals will affirm that the hermeneutical task in regard to Scripture is **interminable** for at least three reasons: 1) because of the continually evolving socio-cultural and personal contexts in which we read Scripture and in which God speaks to us through Scripture; 2) because the intentions of God expressed in his scriptural speech acts are, in keeping with his being,

potentially inexhaustible; but also, 3) because the conceptual-linguistic form of God's revelation to us in Scripture means that we can never lock down its meaning in one exclusive set of timeless propositional truths.

Interpreting Scripture in this postmodern manner further demands of us: 1) sensitivity to the nuances of the text in terms of its **canonical**, literary, grammatical, and historical contexts; 2) careful attention to the wider interpretive community, both locally and generally throughout Christian orthodoxy; and 3) a set of **hermeneutical virtues,** but above all

Interminable here means "endless."

Canon = "rule." *Canonical* refers to the formation of the many books of the Bible into one Scripture or "rule." Here it refers to the many different books of the Bible existing together in one context.

A *virtue* is an acquired disposition to act in a particular manner that is good (e.g., courage or wisdom). *Hermeneutical virtues*, therefore, are acquired dispositions to understand and interpret (or see) texts in certain ways or with particular qualities.

Triangulation refers to any attempt to find a position or location by means of (at least) two other points of reference.

the faith, hope, and love required to recognize and respond in obedience to the illuminating presence and activity of the Holy Spirit. The goal of reading Scripture for its meaning—as opposed to several other appropriate and necessary ways to read Scripture—is not so much to find *the* meaning in the text as it is to, through a process of careful **triangulation** (along the axes of text, community, and tradition),[6] hear the voice of God speak into our present life context through the pages of Scripture. This is not a laissez-faire, free-for-all form of interpretation; neither is it a diminution of the role and status of Scripture as the ultimate source of theology. Rather, postpropositionalism is an attempt to take more seriously the voice of God in Scripture, acknowledging that the same Spirit who speaks in Scripture

Irenaeus' regula fidei refers to the teaching of the apostles (as summarized in the Apostles' Creed). He proposed the *regula fidei* as a way of keeping our interpretation of Scripture orthodox.

Irenaeus was an immensely significant second-century Christian thinker who defended orthodoxy against the Gnostic heresy.

Sola scriptura literally means "Scripture alone." It was one of the central tenets of the Protestant Reformation and refers to Scripture as the only authority for Christian belief and practice.

is vitally at work in our interpretations of it. Ultimately, then, a crucial test for postpropositional interpretation of Scripture concerns the ***regula fidei*** ("rule of faith") of **Irenaeus**, in which we test our interpretations over and against "the faith once for all entrusted to the saints" (Jude 3). I am convinced that at this point in the history of Western Christianity the way to remain faithful to ***sola scriptura*** is to adopt the kind of postpropositional approach I have begun to sketch here.

COMMENTS

THREAD ONE:
(INTER)SUBJECTIVE TRIANGULATION AND INTERPRETATION

- Scot McKnight: **Propositions and the purpose of Scripture**

Myron, many thanks for this. There are about five hundred things to think about when one broaches the "evangelical" theory of "Scripture" and "hermeneutics." I like very much your triangulation, and your swarming it all with the Holy Spirit. There is lots of Grenz and Franke in all this, and they have been lights for many of us.

I would ask this: What is the purpose of Scripture?—for knowing this enables us to sort through some of these issues. And the issue of the linguistic turn is part and parcel of our perception of what Scripture says. I think the language of proposition and postproposition is important, but sometimes gets lost in a tug of war. Isn't the issue the value of our propositions? Their inerrancy or justifiability? The linguistic turn informs us of the impact of the Subject on the Object we are seeking to know and teaches us that, because the Subject does make an impact, our interpretations must be held with—to adapt the Quaker phrase—some "holy hushing." Is this a way around the ["proposition versus no-proposition"] debate?

Again, thanks.

- Myron Bradley Penner: **Scripture makes us "wise unto salvation"**

Scot: Thanks for your comments. . . . I have enjoyed your Jesus Creed blog many times and am honored to have you participate in this conversation. You are right to note the influence of Grenz and Franke on my thinking, particularly with respect to the role of the Holy Spirit. As for your specific points:

First, you make an excellent observation in regard to the importance of what we believe the purpose of Scripture to be, relative to how we construe its nature. Such awareness will certainly help us find our way through some of these issues. As a matter of fact, part of the point in my post—and my blog on postmodern evangelicalism—was to highlight how we evangelicals have (rather unimaginatively) taken Scripture exclusively to concern "propositional revelation," when in fact this doesn't fit well with Scripture's own presentation and commentary about itself. My suggestion is that Scripture is about more than this, and this something more concerns, in the broad strokes, making us "wise unto salvation." There is, of course, more to any given passage than a straightforward concern with **soteriological issues**, and thus we must be open to something more than just information about getting saved, or what have you.

> *Soteriological issues* are theological issues concerning the doctrine of salvation.

Which leads to your second point regarding our evangelical fixation on propositions, and here I couldn't agree with you more. I find your allusion to the Quaker notion of "holy hushing" alluring, if by it you mean to reinstate a sense of mystery into God's speaking in Scripture and a sense that we cannot control the text through any formal procedures. My postpropositional language is meant to indicate something of the sort, only in the meanwhile indicate that one of the things Scripture is doing is giving us something like information with cognitive content. Holy hushing means taking Scripture more seriously than a propositionalist, not less!

- Colin Toffelmire: **Triangulated meaning and (inter)subjective interpretation**

Myron: Good stuff, I must say. I'm particularly interested to hear more on the subject of "careful triangulation" in our interpretation of Scripture. If I'm reading you correctly (and please correct me if I'm not), you're proposing a brand of interpretation that is less concerned with "the correct interpretation" and more concerned with discovering a layer of meaning in the text. I appreciate this line of thinking, and I particularly appreciate the fact that you recognize that many factors must influence our interpretation of any given passage.

I would, however, like to add at least one more factor to the components you mention in your post (my apologies for ruining your excellent triangulation metaphor). Any interpretation must depend not merely upon external factors (e.g., community, text, and tradition), but also upon subjective, internal factors (e.g., personal history, culture, language, belief system, etc.). Every interpretation must be, by definition, subjective to some degree. The great benefit that I see in your three axes is their ability to critique and challenge subjective readings, not by offering "objective" interpretations but by providing other subjective interpretations with which to dialogue. Thus we create interpretations that are not merely subjective, but *inter*subjective: readings that submit to one another. The natural outcome of this (as I see it at least) will be a situation where many (but not all) readings can be accepted as valid and true. Thus any given text may be interpreted in a number of different ways, each with its own measure of validity.

- Myron Bradley Penner: **Intersubjective triangulation and the myth of objectivity**

Colin: I entirely agree with what you're saying and was thinking much along the lines you suggest. In fact, the phrase "careful triangulation" in my original version was "intersubjective triangulation." Another of the things I accept about the **pomo** critique of modernity is what I call "the myth of objectivity"—along with a few of the other modern myths, such as the myth of progress and the myth of epistemic infallibility. I would further point to

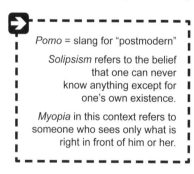

Pomo = slang for "postmodern"

Solipsism refers to the belief that one can never know anything except for one's own existence.

Myopia in this context refers to someone who sees only what is right in front of him or her.

Kierkegaard's "subjectivity principle" as providing us with a rubric in which subjectivity (i.e., subjective involvement) becomes the means and precondition for any meaningful "objectivity." My phrase, "intersubjective triangulation" (which I now regret editing out), is meant to capture what you describe; namely that there is no realm of pure objectivity and yet a **solipsistic** and **myopic** fixation on self leads into all sorts of error (and, indeed, relativism and subjectivism). Thanks for giving me the opportunity to clarify this!

THREAD TWO:
VIRTUE, INTERPRETATION, AND MARGINAL VOICES

• Jonathan Wood: **Virtues and hermeneutics?**

Dr. Penner, thanks a lot for the thought-provoking entry. I am especially interested in the inclusion of (ethical) virtues within your postmodern biblical hermeneutics. This seems to me to be the most interesting possibility to a "post-propositional" hermeneutic.

My questions to you are 1) How exactly do you see these virtues fleshed out within the act of biblical interpretation? and 2) Do you have any thoughts on the place of these virtues within a more general hermeneutic framework?

• Myron Bradley Penner: **The Bible and hermeneutical virtues**

Jonathan: As always, your questions get right to the nitty-gritty. In response to your questions:

1. You wrote: "How exactly do you see these virtues fleshed out within the act of biblical interpretation?"

I don't have it "exactly" figured, but the general picture I have of the role of virtues in biblical interpretation is to see them in lieu of our wider life of Christian virtue. This is in keeping with my above point to Colin in regard to the inherently subjective nature of all our cognitive acts. This means that our cognitive acts are an intrinsic part of our moral life, not acci-dentally through their **entailments**, etc. In other words, ethics applies directly to the thoughts and ideas we have directly—so that they are good or bad—and not just be-cause they are derived from some source that is deemed good or bad.

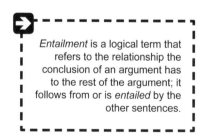

Entailment is a logical term that refers to the relationship the conclusion of an argument has to the rest of the argument; it follows from or is *entailed* by the other sentences.

Several other thoughts: 1) I see vir-tues as connected with forms of life. Simply put, our understanding of certain concepts means that we know what we can and cannot do with them within our linguistic community. Biblical interpretation, then, is not disconnected from our sharing certain practices, forms of life, etc., as Christians and our felicitously engaging in them. 2) Understanding Scripture, like understanding anyone else, is not a mechanical or formulaic process, but requires *discernment*—an attribute which, when used by Christians in relation to Scripture, requires the further activity of the Holy Spirit. 3) We must treat Scripture (in one sense) like any other human speech act. A fundamental part of our verbal interactions with other humans is that we treat the person's words as if they are closely connected to that person—so that if we ignore their words, or twist them, etc., we are ethically responsible to those persons for our actions. We must treat Scripture as the speech act of God (and its human authors). The whole situation is considerably more complex, but I think we need to realize that our biblical interpretations are not entirely different morally and ethically than our interpretations of other human beings.

2. You wrote: "Do you have any thoughts on the place of these virtues within a more general hermeneutic framework?"

Again, I do not have any detailed "system" worked out, and have only some preparatory thoughts on the general subject of hermeneutical virtues. In addition to what I said in answer to your first question, I would also note the hermeneutical primacy of the Christian virtue of love. Obviously, there are other virtues with hermeneutical value (like humility, courage, etc.), but over all these hermeneutical virtues we must put on love—not just so we behave well toward the people we are interpreting (so, for example, we don't yell at them, or what have you), but also so that we truly understand them.

• Len: **Love and authority**

By the way, Scot McKnight raises the question of whether the word *authority* describes the [authority-]relationship as we actually practice it. [Editors' note: We're not sure what Len is referring to, as Scot does not raise this question in his comments here. Perhaps this is a reference to one of Scot's published works.] This is another area where modern epistemic views have constrained us. I recall St. Anselm's **credo ut intelligam** vs. St. Bernard's **credo ut experiar**. I believe in order to experience—or, more dynamically, to love. Love is the lens we are reaching for here, and the missing element in too many discussions of epistemology. To love God is to know God and to hear him and participate and partner with him. It is to be in covenant. If I have to start talking about my authority in my marriage, something has already gone wrong.

> *credo ut intelligam* = "I believe in order to understand." St. Anselm was an important medieval philosopher, often referred to as the father of Scholasticism.
>
> *credo ut experiar* = "I believe in order to experience." St. Bernard of Clairvaux was a conservative and highly influential twelfth-century monk.

• Ellen Haroutunian: **Virtues and openness to marginalized voices**

Thanks, Myron, for a discussion which invites us anew to the beauty, power, and diverse nature of the Scriptures. Within the modern approach to the Scripture there has been an assumed interpretive authority which has limited or even excluded the voices of those who are not from the dominant interpretive culture. The postpropositional perspective makes room for other forms of interpretation to be considered. Cultures that are rich in narrative tradition, women, and people groups who have as a piece of their identity the experience of being the "excluded other" all long to come to the scriptural texts to find their stories reflected within a redemptive hermeneutic. As you have said, we can open up to "accommodate the different ways in which Scripture is true." We rightly have been wary of a too subjective reading of the text, but I wonder if a broader hermeneutical community will not only diminish the errors of an isolated reading but also enrich our interpretation as we listen to how Jesus reveals himself uniquely to each of us. I would like to see more attention paid to a narrative hermeneutic as well. We are all stories.

I love your statement, "We must treat Scripture as the speech act of God (and its human authors). The whole situation is considerably more complex, but I think we need to realize that our biblical interpretations are not entirely different morally and ethically than our interpretations of other human beings." I would add that the way we read the Scriptures is the way we read our lives and the way we read each other, and vice versa. I had a professor who used to say, "Show me how you read your Bible, and I'll show you how you love." We have a "hermeneutic of life" that impacts how we live in relationships on many levels. A propositional reading of Scripture has allowed us to stand over the text in authority, keeping it tamed within our boundaries. A propositional reading of people and community has crushed many broken reeds.

To open ourselves to faith, hope, and love, we must learn to come to the Scriptures in a way that allows our presuppositions, propositions, and convictions to be addressed and challenged, not reinforced. Our mythical objectivity has kept us safe from the two-edged sword. I do agree that there is a healthy and necessary place for the literary-historical-grammatical context in our approach. Perhaps we are becoming simpler again on the "other side" of complex. I have a friend who, when teaching hermeneutics, asks the entire class to get on their knees and ask God's help to "see" and "hear" what God desires to reveal in the text. It's a bit dramatic, yes, but the point is well made. To allow Scripture to speak (and to live in genuine love relationship with God and each other), we need to move from a mastering scrutiny to a receptive wonder. As you pointed out, it is the *logos* himself whom we are hoping to meet.

• Eric Mason: **Artistic interpretation and minorities**

The exciting aspect of the values you articulated for a postpropositional interpretation of Scripture is the possibilities for creativity in narration and performance of Scripture. By releasing Scripture from some of the modern critical theories that have bound individual interpretation, there is the opportunity for dramatic and revolutionary responses to Scripture that might have otherwise been considered radical. The key is rooted now not in the translation and semantics but in the dynamic reaction of the listener as the listener "triangulates" his or her hearing into a practical response of obedience. We become participants of a performance, a performance of characters (the dynamic of text and community) and set (community and tradition) and script (tradition and text). (We are not dealing with stolid columns of propositions now but dynamic, living vortexes of activity.) But as each performance is unique to the performers and altered by the audience, the orthodoxy of the author's intent becomes the guiding directorial influence.

[I have one concern with your emphasis on the hermeneutical virtues of faith, hope, and love.] The struggle I see here is a faith struggle for the church. This seems deeply rooted in apologetics. How does the establishment respond to minority interpretations? How can the postpropositional church **catholic** continue to practice orthodoxy and communicate orthodoxy without the effect of entropy and the encroachment of false teaching?

You have suggested what amounts to two correcting influences on our future church: 1) the triangulation of text, community, and tradition; and 2) "the illuminating presence and activity of the Holy Spirit." Sprinkling upon these two correcting influences a heaping dose of generosity and humility, we must rely heavily upon faith in God's sovereignty and the living activity of the Holy Spirit to actively punish and exterminate heresy and false teaching. God will handle the keeping of his kingdom. He is a territorial lion. I believe that if we are an obedient church we will see little heresy. The trouble has been a historical lack of obedience in the church and in individual persons. If our communities are actively engaging in obedience as a response to Scripture and the impetus of the Holy Spirit, we will constantly be renewing a kingdom ethos that, by its nature, rejects heresy. Why? Because the obedient living out of the commands of our King naturally drives the culture of the community, and heresy will stand out like an **anachronism**—like when an actor walks on the stage in an Elizabethan costume wearing a Timex on her arm.

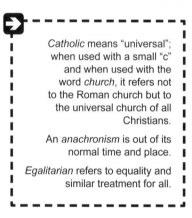

Catholic means "universal"; when used with a small "c" and when used with the word *church*, it refers not to the Roman church but to the universal church of all Christians.

An *anachronism* is out of its normal time and place.

Egalitarian refers to equality and similar treatment for all.

- Colin Toffelmire: **Authorial intention and heresy hunting**

Cheers, Eric; that was good stuff. A couple of points, though. Firstly, I don't think it's fair to say that the interpretive key to Scripture has in fact shifted from "translation and semantics" (from which I take you to mean the semantics, grammar, and syntax of the text itself) to "the dynamic reaction of the listener." I would prefer to think that the tyranny of the former has given way to a more **egalitarian** relationship where the listener/reader is a more active participant in the communicative relationship. Or, even better, the listener/reader now *realizes* how active a participant in interpretation s/he always was. The grammatical/syntactical relationships in the text still matter because all human communication is an attempt to be maximally relevant, even to the point of using complex grammar to make subtle points (see W. J. Lyons and J. M. Blackwell, *Un/Limited Indeterminacy: Biblical Interpretation of the Acts of the Apostles*, University of Sheffield, for more on this idea).

My other question/comment was concerning your hope that "the orthodoxy of the author's intent" will become "the guiding directorial influence" in a reader/ listener (community?) centered interpretation. But how, then, can we know the author's intent? How can we be sure that the orthodoxy we are reading is not simply our own "orthodoxy" being mirrored back at us from within the text as we bring all of our baggage to it? It strikes me that your comments regarding minority interpretation suggest that you realize the problem.

[This] leads to my final question: How do we know when God is weeding out heresy and we are being obedient? It seems to me that there have been many times in history when the church has been working to be obedient and that obedience has resulted in violence against others for the sake of orthodoxy. How do we know whether such actions were from God or from humans? When you suggest God as the guardian of our orthodoxy, how will he guard it: using people or with lightning from heaven? I'm not trying to be facetious; I think this is a legitimate issue to discuss. I suppose the question as I would pose it is: How then shall we be orthodox? Blessings.

• Eric Mason: **Identifying heresy through communal consensus**

It is said that Greek sailors in the classical period would attend theater festivals while in port. During those events, the sailors had a method by which they would watch dramas so closely that they were able to perform them nearly word for word on their ships later when at sea. How?

In many native cultures that had no or only rudimentary written language there are stories of members of those cultures being able to recite whole passages of written text after only a single hearing. In fact, there are documented reports of Native American tribes being able to recite whole treaties from memory when

US officials met with them to alter their treaty agreements. How were they able to do this?

The actor/audience/author relationship is a dynamic one. There is what was said (the script), there is what happened (the plot), there is who said it and who did it (the characters). Those dynamic triangles are corrective by their nature, like the angles of a shape that can never equal more than 180 degrees. But the audience response is dynamic, as is the presentation of the production. If a response or a presentation run counter to the original intent of the author, you are right in assuming there are two corrective forces that come into play: those who have seen the play and the author himself. I do not know how the author will correct the truth. But I know that many of us know him and can tell you at least in part what he is like. And I know that when there are many hearers the treaty is remembered and the play can be performed. Why? Because when someone gets it wrong there are a hundred voices that rise to say, "No, he said it more like this. . . ." "Yes, and then she said. . . ."

I also believe that a community of obedient (nasty word) followers of Jesus will know heresy when they hear it. Like I said, it will be like an anachronism, an anomaly, a snake in the grass.

As for the idea that translation and semantics are no longer the key to interpretation, well, I think I stick by that. If you were to try to find a **Rosetta stone** for this age, I think that it would be rooted in the outcome rather than the words themselves. Our quest for the perfect translation for this culture is, in the end, futile. We are a long way from *gay* and *loins* meaning

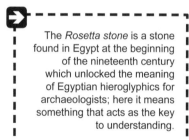

The *Rosetta stone* is a stone found in Egypt at the beginning of the nineteenth century which unlocked the meaning of Egyptian hieroglyphics for archaeologists; here it means something that acts as the key to understanding.

what they did [in past generations]. And we will be a long way from *happy* and *heart* tomorrow. Essentially, then, it is the response that gives us the proper key to interpretation. The transmission becomes flexible and mobile and adaptable. But the receiver becomes the key to the cipher. Do we understand the orders and then obey them? Do I?

- Colin Toffelmire: **Understanding by obeying**

Hey Eric, this is in reply to your post about the actor/audience/author relationship. I fully agree that this is generally the case. There is some kind of instinctual, almost unconscious knowledge or sense that helps us as a church to guide each other. But does that sense always work? Is it universally effective? In your system is it ever possible for the lone dissenting voice to be right? And how do we know?

As for the bit about translation, I think we might be talking across each other. I'm not talking about the semantics found in various English translations of Scripture, or choosing between various translations. What I meant to say is that when we are reading, interpreting, and translating in Hebrew, Greek, and Aramaic, grammar and syntax are tremendously important due to the human propensity to communicate as well as possible at all times.

[You asked:] Do we understand the orders and then obey them? I dunno [*sic*], maybe we come to understand the orders by obeying them. Cheers.

- Myron Bradley Penner: **Objectively risky faith and marginal voices**

Eric: Some great stuff of your own! And in particular, I enjoy being read carefully. You have understood my comments substantively in the way I understand them. You have a cluster of concerns and I will try to address most of them.

I recognize your concern about silencing marginal voices and take it very seriously. As I see it, the postpropositionalist perspective I am adopting entails that the activity of biblical interpretation—and just the Christian faith in general—is a much more objectively risky affair. We have to venture out over **Kierkegaard's 70,000 fathoms of water**. This means that we will have to take some interpretive risks as well. We must always leave ourselves open to God's extraordinary (prophetic) working in an individual's life to correct his church. However, it is one thing for an individual to take risks and quite another for "the establishment" to do so. The church must faithfully proclaim the

> Søren Kierkegaard famously defined faith as being "suspended over 70,000 fathoms of water," in order to highlight the inherent riskiness of faith.

Word of God that it has received. It will of necessity need to be patient, humble, and loving in its response to minority interpretations, leaving room to be challenged, but it must be able to determine

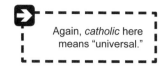

Again, *catholic* here means "universal."

when an interpretation has crossed the bounds of the apostolic gospel. It does this dialectically through a careful listening to **catholic** voices on the issue.

• Eric Mason: **Living exegesis**

Thanks for the response, Dr. Penner. That is much the way I see it as well. I think your saying that "we will have to take some interpretive risks" is enough to give many a modernist cause to fire off an apologetic discourse on the fundamentals. But I say "hurrah"! Too many a church has lost the "objectively risky affair" that reading the inspired Word of God ought to be. Reading Scripture is dangerous business. Interpreting it ought to get us killed. Lives are at stake.

But here I just keep going back to something you said in your initial blog that resonates with the practical minister in me: We must "recognize and respond in obedience to the illuminating presence and activity of the Holy Spirit." I really think this must be at the heart of the postmodern hermeneutic, just as you do. "Responding in obedience" will take us into a living exegesis that I believe, by faith, will result in the expansion of the kingdom. Doing this will root out heresy by building an ethos and a culture of God-truth, something that cannot be subjectively accessed with any certainty but can be objectively transcendent when the source of the truth is truth himself.

When we are interpreting and then obeying as honestly as our sinful hearts can, the postmodern church will be far better apologists. I think you are right on the money. I can't wait to celebrate the risky interpretations and those who are obediently living them out. Those obedient people will easily "be able to determine when an interpretation has crossed the bounds of the apostolic gospel." Those are the ones who I hope will tap a dangerous finger on my shoulder when I go astray and say to me, "What are you doing talking to that snake? He's selling bad dope, man."

THREAD THREE:
SOLA SCRIPTURA AND CHURCH TRADITION

• Chad Sundin: ***Sola scriptura* ain't so *sola***

I'd like to offer what may be a step beyond the ending point of Dr. Penner's [blog]. . . . I'm doubtful that the place Myron's argument really deposits us is one wherein a reaffirmation of the doctrine of *sola scriptura* in any meaningful sense is possible. *Sola scriptura*, as a doctrine of the Reformation, is a declaration about the authority of Scripture over the church. That is, it is meant to be a direct contradiction of the ancient understanding that God's authority on earth is given to the church. It locates that authority in Scripture, and in "Scripture alone." It's in the aftermath of this move that such topics as inerrancy are born and that such discussions as Dr. Penner's about inerrancy's shortcomings are held.

But what if *sola scriptura* was denied outright? What if the text of Scripture was made subject to, or at least held in balance with, other authority-bearing entities so that God's authority is never found in "Scripture alone" but always in "Scripture together with?" I think such a perspective might read an awful lot like Myron's last paragraph (minus the last sentence, of course) if we understand that it is by "interpreting Scripture" that meaning and therefore authority are made possible (i.e., without interpretation the Scriptures are just symbols on a page).

Now as for what those other authority-bearing entities might be, I think Dr. Penner hinted at that with his "triangulation" method of extracting meaning from Scripture: the axes of text, community, and tradition. Or to put it differently: Scripture, tradition (or belief/practice, or the rule of faith preserved by the church), and reason (or that which is from ourselves, embodied as we are in various concentric circles of linguistic, economic, geopolitical, etc. association—i.e., communities—which are animated by the Spirit of God), held in balance, are bearers of God's authority. Not *sola scriptura*.

• Myron Bradley Penner: **Reformers, not revolutionaries**

To Chad: You bring out a very important point, and I quite like your "Scripture together with" idea. Insofar as *sola scriptura* is taken as an "It's just me and

Jesus and my Bible—that's all I need" kind of attitude, then my post unequivocally does away with *sola scriptura*. This, however, is not how I understand the Reformers—at least in their context. The fundamental point the Reformers were driving home with *sola scriptura* is that: 1) the Church of Rome and its papacy did not constitute a second source of revelation; and 2) the Holy Spirit lives in and illuminates the hearts and minds of all believers, and therefore the laity do not need the priesthood to interpret Scripture for them (a flip side of the priesthood of believers argument). The Reformers (at least at first) were not revolutionaries trying to start a new church, but were calling the church back to fidelity to her own tradition. For example, Calvin, for all his talk about the self-interpreting nature of Scripture and the hermeneutical necessity of the Holy Spirit, nonetheless quotes extensively and authoritatively Augustine, the **patristics**, and even scholastic exegetes to support his interpretations of Scripture!

The Reformers' emphasis on *sola scriptura*, then, need not be taken to exclude something like Irenaeus' *regula fidei*, in which tradition operates not as a source of revelation but as an authoritative guide or rule for interpretation. The distinction may be subtle, but I think it is important. It allows for your "Scripture together with" model. The point of the last sentence in my blog, regarding postpropositionalism being the way to remain faithful to *sola scriptura* today, is to signal that the cultural and theological context has changed since the days of the Reformation and our correctives ought not run in the same direction as theirs.

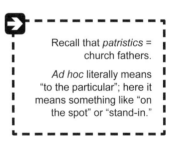

Recall that *patristics* = church fathers.

Ad hoc literally means "to the particular"; here it means something like "on the spot" or "stand-in."

• Chad Sundin: ***Sola scriptura* is/was not faithful to tradition**

Myron, I appreciate your perspective on the context in which the Reformers were advocating *sola scriptura*. I must admit, my reading of Reformation theology is mostly from secondary sources, of which you are now a favorite. So, with you as my **ad hoc** authority on the Reformers' contextual emphases, I still think *sola scriptura* is a doctrine we should politely dismiss on the grounds that it is less than helpful in realizing the goal of "calling the church back to fidelity to her own tradition."

You wrote that the points the Reformers were driving home with *sola scriptura* were 1) that Rome and her papacy did not constitute a source of revelation and 2) that the Holy Spirit is in each believer as a hermeneutical guide, and therefore **lay folks** don't need priests for interpretation. I think both of these points are valid with reference to the specific issues facing the Reformers, but not much further.

Regarding the first point: Yes, the geopolitical entity, complete with army and king and treaties, that was the Church of Rome at the end of the Middle Ages needed to be called to a higher standard than the pope's mandate. But the Reformers' concept of "revelation," or "special revelation," as being confined to the canon of Holy Scripture doesn't seem to jibe with the more fluid understanding of revelation that existed during the few hundred years on either side of the events of the New Testament. One example of this in the Jewish world that Jesus participated in is his famous preface, "You have heard it said _____, but I say to you _____."

> *Lay folks* is a reference to the "laity," which means those in the church who are not ordained ministers.
>
> The *Talmud* is the oral tradition of Judaism, a written record of the discussion of rabbis on Jewish law, ethics, customs, and history that became the basis of many rabbinic laws and customs. Traditionally Jews believe that, as a commentary on the written Law, the Talmud is a source of revelation parallel to the Torah, which (like the Torah) has its origins in Moses's encounter with Yahweh (God) on Mt. Sinai.

This phrase was not unique to Jesus, but rather was the standard preface by which special, authority-bearing teachers could offer authoritative, corrective interpretations of the Hebrew Scriptures for the purpose of bringing people into obedience with them. (I'm not making claims here about whether or not Jesus' teachings were conventional or fully unique, so don't let that bother you.)

Now on the face of it, this approach—rabbis speaking with authority to establish right belief and practice—seems consistent with Irenaeus—the tradition of the church as a rule to interpretation of Scripture; but, in fact, it goes beyond that to something that quite resembles "revelation." In Jewish and in Christian history during the first few centuries AD, we see the teachings and practical instructions of elders/rabbinical sages on the one hand and church fathers/bishops on the other being regarded as sacred revelation: not on the same level as the Scriptures, but within the bounds of being divinely inspired and authoritative. For Jews, these teachings were compiled into the **Talmud**. For Christians, the creeds and sacraments, among other things, were considered to be from God himself. So yes, the late medieval papacy needed a corrective, and the "no new revelation" aspect of *sola scriptura* served as that in its context, but it doesn't seem to have brought the church "back to fidelity to her own tradition."

Regarding the second point: There was a clear need [for the Reformers] to take divine interpretation out of the sole possession of the professional, certified, and formally authorized priesthood. But by making individuals the bearers of divine inspiration enough that, through the Holy Spirit in them, each person needs no other human authority to interpret Scripture (even if Calvin didn't put this belief into practice), again, I think the Reformers were off the point. The concept of the self from which the Reformers operated seems to me to have the opposite locus of identity to the earliest Christians (and basically their whole contemporary world). For them, by my secondary accounts, the self is identified first as an individual and [then, secondly, in relation to others]. So for the Reformers, if the Holy Spirit resides in the church in any meaningful sense, the Holy Spirit resides in each individual soul. But the earliest Christians would have derived their individual identity from the group to which they belonged. So for the early Christians, the Holy Spirit dwells in the church, of which individuals are a part. An individual, then, as a part of the corporate body, can partake of the Spirit that dwells in the church. Now, of course, the specifics of how this understanding of the self and the Holy Spirit's interaction with it as that interaction pertains to interpreting Scripture is a huge discussion. All I want to say about it is that in this understanding the Spirit's guidance of the individual is a function of the Spirit's guidance of the church. So however *sola scriptura* was played out in the context of an interpretational monopoly by clergy, I don't think it was a move "back to fidelity to [the church's] own tradition" in this regard either.

So again, I still don't think *sola scriptura*, even in the light you shine on it, is worth remaining faithful to. I don't think your postpropositionalism needs it as a reference, and I don't think it's a good way to "reform back to" anything other than some distinctly modern errors, even if they were used by God in their context.

- Myron Bradley Penner: **Getting over the Reformation?**

Chad: In regard to your first point about Jewish approaches to Scripture, I am not convinced we're getting the whole picture; neither do I see the straight line from Jewish practices and beliefs to Christian practices and beliefs that you seem to see. In other words, while Christians certainly should be mindful of Jewish beliefs and practices, and can learn much of value to their Christian faith from them, the issue of the normativity of Judaism for Christians is . . . well . . . complex, to say the least. I am definitely *not* an expert in **Second Temple Judaism**, and there

> *Second Temple Judaism* refers to Jewish belief and practice during Jesus' time, during the time of the second temple of Jerusalem (515 BC to 70 AD).
>
> A *Midrash* is something like a Jewish biblical commentary.
>
> *Torah* is the Jewish word for the Law of Moses or the Pentateuch—the first five books of the Bible (Genesis, Exodus, Leviticus, Numbers, and Deuteronomy). Traditionally, for Jews this is the literal word of God as dictated to Moses.

is a great deal of complexity surrounding the Jewish Scriptures concerning the **Midrashim**, the Talmud, and the **Torah**. Debating these issues—for example, whether the Jews of Jesus' day really believed that the Talmud was God's Word in the same sense as the Torah—would be something of a dead end anyway, to my mind. I for one am not ready to admit that church councils, creeds, etc. are inviolate, and I cannot think of a sufficient motivation to do so—particularly in light of the diversity and fragmentation of Christian traditions. To my mind, church councils, creeds, etc. express, in their better moments, the best way to articulate God's revelation within a particular human context.

In the end, I do not think appealing to Jewish practice will help save you from traditional evangelical bibliology either. One argument evangelical inerrantists will often make, for example, is that their view of Scripture is the same as Second Temple Judaism (and therefore Jesus' view as well), and therefore the doctrine of inerrancy is neither a twentieth-century invention nor unbiblical. You are right to say that the Jews had a much higher view of tradition than the typical evangelical, and I agree that we can and must see God speaking by his Spirit in and through the consensus of his people; but, in my understanding, there is room for a distinction between the Word of God and the authority of tradition—a distinction I find in Irenaeus' rule of faith.

As for your second point about the Reformers' individualism, I agree with you that there is an extreme danger today of our interpreting *sola scriptura*, and just the Reformation in general, in terms of **modern notions about the self**, but I think we may be guilty of an anachronism if we impute that view to the Protestant Reformers themselves. That is to say, the Reformers were not good modernists, nor were they Cartesian philosophers. I agree that the Reformation fed the fires of individualism and functioned in tandem with other philosophical and social developments to produce our current state of affairs; but I doubt whether the Reformers' views of self, taken on their own, should be read as starkly individualistic. They certainly believed that the Holy Spirit indwelt individual persons, but this was not in isolation from the Spirit's indwelling of the church, as you suggest.

And I simply do not think it is the case that early Christians derived their identity from the church irrespective of their individual standing to God in Christ, or that they believed they received the Holy Spirit from being united to the church rather than Christ dwelling in them individually by the power of the Holy Spirit. It was their individual indwelling by Christ through the Spirit, and their subsequent and personal power and gifting by the Spirit, which united early Christians to their fellow believers. At the same time, it was their corporate experience together, with the mutual indwelling by the Spirit, which enabled early Christians to understand their new identity as an identity together with the other **called-out ones**. In other words, I think that it is a both-and: the early church believed *both* that they had been individually indwelt by the Holy Spirit *and* that the Holy Spirit indwelled them all together as the corporate entity of the church.

> For more on modern notions of the self, see Blog 1.
>
> The favorite New Testament word for church is *ecclesia*, which means "called-out ones."

All of this is to say that I still believe in the spirit of *sola scriptura* as I believe the Reformers meant it: in concert with Irenaeus' rule of faith. However, I am in agreement with your point that the importance of the specific character of their reformation was relative to a situation that now largely does not exist anymore. So maybe it's time to get over (at least certain aspects of) the Reformation!

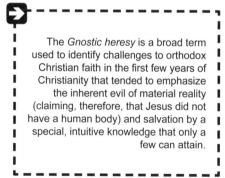

EVANGELICAL FAITH
AND (POSTMODERN) OTHERS

Mabiala Kenzo

For many, evangelical faith and postmodernism make strange bedfellows. Some evangelicals, in fact, see in the postmodern culture of pluralism "the ugly face" of "the most dangerous threat to the gospel since the rise of the **Gnostic heresy** in the second century."[1] And yet, with its mutation from a largely Western phenomenon to a global phenomenon, evangelical faith needs to contend with postmodernism in a more perceptive way, for the new evangelicals are likely to see the postmodern "intense distrust of all universal or 'totalizing' discourses"[2] as a much-needed emancipation from "the 'monotony' of universal modernism's vision of the world."[3] The question we must ask ourselves is: How is evangelical faith (in its Western expression) going to deal with its other, non-Western expressions that are admittedly postmodern?

> The *Gnostic heresy* is a broad term used to identify challenges to orthodox Christian faith in the first few years of Christianity that tended to emphasize the inherent evil of material reality (claiming, therefore, that Jesus did not have a human body) and salvation by a special, intuitive knowledge that only a few can attain.

Postmodernism is susceptible to many constructions. As an epistemic alternative, it embodies belief in the

vernacular, "with pluralism, borders and multiple perspectives being highlighted as a means of disrupting the centralizing impulse of any system."[4] Hence the resulting postmodern condition defines itself in terms of "**hybridity**," "incoherence," "indetermination," "plurality," "contextuality," and "lack of one single organizing principle." Its ethos wages "war on totality" and the **hegemony** of any single perspective, while encouraging and celebrating the regional, the local, the particular, and indeed the vernacular. It is as such that many non-Western thinkers embrace postmodernism as a way of liberation from "the extraordinary **hubris** of modernism,"[5] which seeks to master **being** by forcing it into a **binary opposition** of "same/other, spirit/matter, subject/object, inside/outside, pure/impure, rational/chaotic."[6] Two additional features of postmodernism justify its attraction to non-Westerners. First, instead of the stability of the universal rule of reason that the Enlightenment paradigm promises, postmodernism encourages and celebrates hybridity, **pastiche**, **mimicry**, and **bricolage**, which are familiar notions to non-Western intellectual traditions. Second, against the modernist contempt for anything traditional, postmodernism, which has been defined as a recuperative strategy of the past,[7] encourages and celebrates the traditional that it recuperates in its own construal of reality.

Yet non-Westerners have not embraced postmodernism uncritically. In fact, some non-Westerners warn against the dangers of postmodernism, pointing out that it constitutes "the condition of knowledge in the most highly developed societies."[8] To embrace it would therefore lead to the most extreme form of alienation.

> ➡
>
> *Vernacular* = common, everyday language; sometimes used (as it is here) to refer to something that is derived from the ordinary and common.
>
> *Hybridity* refers to a composite of different types of things (or ideas) from different sources.
>
> *Hegemony* = exclusive control
>
> *Hubris* refers to extreme pride or arrogance.
>
> *Being* in this context is a philosophical category used to refer to the essence of all that is. To "master being," then, is to control reality.
>
> *Binary opposition* refers to two ideas or words that are exact opposites.
>
> *Pastiche* literally refers to a composite work made up from different mediums and genres.
>
> *Mimicry* = copying ideas, concepts, language, etc. from someone else.
>
> *Bricolage* means something like "making it up from scratch," without following preestablished rules.

Moreover, even where postmodernism seems to critique the universalist pretensions of the Western **episteme**, it still surreptitiously serves its cause in that it ends up "not with its dispersal into local vernaculars but with a return to another First World language with universalist epistemological pretensions."[9] Finally, by deconstructing the subject by causing it to peter out in an endless dissemination of meaning, postmodernism seals the death of the very subjects it seeks to liberate.

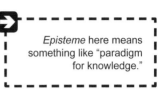

Episteme here means something like "paradigm for knowledge."

Yet, despite these strong objections, postmodernism continues to hold sway over non-Westerners. The reason, in my view, resides in the fact that the non-Westerners have almost no credible alternative to postmodernism. Of course, they might be tempted either to fall back on the modern representation of the non-Western in "the colonial library"[10] or to appeal to their premodern and precolonial past. Unfortunately, the first alternative falls short because modern discourse on the non-Western world is not innocent. Despite the scientific mantle with which it wraps itself, colonial discourse is nothing but "European" constructions intended to maintain power over non-Europeans.[11] As V. Y. Mudimbe and Edward Said argue, the West invented Africa and the Orient to serve as the Other of the West.[12] The second alternative, which consists in reclaiming the premodern or precolonial past of Africa, is also futile, for one cannot underestimate the extent to which the global South has been impacted by the colonial experience. The gap that stands between the present and the precolonial past is unbridgeable.

Given the difficulties that these alternatives represent, it is no wonder that postmodernism is embraced as an ally in the struggle for local and vernacular identities throughout the non-Western world. To be sure, one does not necessarily encounter the influence of postmodernism on non-Westerners under that name. In fact, most non-Westerners seem to prefer to use the term post*colonialism* to describe the struggle for identity in the non-Western cultural context today. Those non-Western thinkers who have embraced the notion of postcolonialism join hands with all those who, wherever they may be found, are seeking to come to terms with the experience of colonization and its aftermath. Postmodernism turns out to be an ally of postcolonialism in that those who are seeking to come to terms with the experience of colonization and its long-term effects see in postmodernism not only the possibility of an alternative discourse that affirms and celebrates otherness, but also a strategy for the "deconstruction of the concept, the authority, and assumed primacy of the category of 'the West.'"[13] Hence, despite the risks involved, the appeal to postmodernism has become a necessity for non-Westerners. It is no longer a luxury, but a matter of "to be or not to be."

Postmodern strategies have also made their way into non-Western theological practices through postcolonial theologies. These theologies, which are essentially discourses of otherness, embody the desire on the part of those who produce them to exercise what Tite Tiénou calls "the right to difference."[14] As theologies of otherness and difference, they embody "agonistic," (that is, primarily negative) relations of competition, opposition, and even repression with respect to Western Christian theologies. They constitute themselves as voices of otherness and seek to articulate the margins or what has been projected as marginal; they take "hold not only of actual power, but also of the languages, systems of metaphors and regimes of images that seem designed to silence those whom they embody in representation."[15]

Theology in a postcolonial context is a highly political affair. Postcolonial theologies will not settle for a position at the margins of their Western counterparts. Rather, they surreptitiously seek to turn the margin into the center, thereby disrupting the serenity grounded on the assumption that Western formulations are self-evident. In so doing they display a great deal of creativity, a creativity whose theoretical framework is the postmodern concepts of pastiche, *bricolage*, mimicry, hybridity, and **play**. One catches a glimpse of this creativity in theological projects that have recently come out of Africa, in which classical **Christological** categories inherited from **Chalcedon** are reopened to make room for African ones. The result is a hybridized Christology where Christ is worshiped as "Chief" (Kabasele), "Ancestor" (Pobee, Bujo, Bediako, and Nyamiti), "Master of initiation" (Sanon), "Healer" (Kolié), or "Elder Brother" (Kabasele).

> *Play* in this context means deliberately and obviously breaking with the norms or "rules" of language or society in order to demonstrate that they are not absolute.
>
> *Christology* is the doctrine of Jesus Christ.
>
> The Council of Chalcedon (451 AD) articulated the orthodox position on Christ's two natures.

Evangelical faith encounters in postcolonial theology what it always wanted: a **contextual theology** for the so-called Third World. Indeed, for many years evangelicals have championed the cause of a self-theologizing church, which they argued is the fourth woefully needed addition to the classical three-selves of the indigenous church (self-governing, self-supporting, and self-propagating). In postcolonial theologies, their dream has finally come true. The (**subaltern**) latecomer has finally spoken in her own native **idiom**. Evangelical faith, which has hitherto been articulated and formulated in the stable idiom of Western rationalism that guaran-

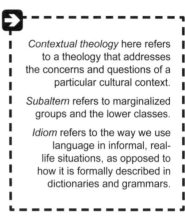

Contextual theology here refers to a theology that addresses the concerns and questions of a particular cultural context.

Subaltern refers to marginalized groups and the lower classes.

Idiom refers to the way we use language in informal, real-life situations, as opposed to how it is formally described in dictionaries and grammars.

teed its sameness, suddenly finds itself confronted with other idioms that disturb both the stability of classical formulations and the appeal of sameness.

Will evangelical faith break or stretch? Therein lies the question.

COMMENTS

- Sivin Kit: **Affirmation from a fellow non-Westerner**

This post really caught my attention. I found this a refreshing perspective, perhaps because it takes into consideration a non-Western perspective, which I'm also part of, and a postcolonial touch, which I can also identify with.

- DangerMouse: **Strange bedfellows indeed**

Personally, I just don't get it. I find it very hard to understand how (in my perspective) one manages to perform the mental gymnastics to hold an evangelical faith and postmodern belief in the same brain. I gave up a while ago—however, it may not be true that I was ever evangelical in the first place. However, despite my lack of comprehension, I am sure that [holding an evangelical faith *and* postmodern belief] is important. *Bon courage* to all who take that path.

- Brian McLaren: **We need ears that hear the Other**

I want to stand up and cheer for Kenzo's posting. I have been hoping that someone from the global South (i.e., the world colonized and exploited by Europeans) would articulate these things. It is hard for me to imagine his posting being improved upon. As another reader said, it bears reading and rereading.

I have been wondering more and more over the last few years if I should stop using the word *postmodern* altogether and only use the word *postcolonial* instead. Kenzo's posting articulates why I have felt this way. In many ways, I believe at the heart of European postmodern thought has been a kind of repentance for the atrocities of colonialism. (It is not insignificant that Jacques Derrida was a Jew, a citizen of France, born in Algeria—then a French colony.) As thoughtful European intellectuals began assessing the fruits of the modern Western mindset,

I believe they wanted to somehow weaken it so it would do less damage. (See my posting in Blog One Comments in reply to Bruce Benson's Blog One piece for more on this, including an acknowledgement of the incompleteness of this response.) Their motivation was, in this sense, far from being the licentious moral relativism for which they are often caricatured, but profoundly moral.

One could only wish that we who claim to be followers of Jesus—who was crucified by a colonial superpower in collusion with a civil religion—would have been sensitive to these matters far earlier than we were, and far more than we are. (Sadly, many of us are still almost completely insensitive to them.)

If some readers of European descent don't understand why colonialism is so significant, can I recommend they study the story of Kenzo's home country? Adam Hochschild's *King Leopold's Ghost: A Story of Greed, Terror, and Heroism in Colonial Africa* (New York: Houghton Mifflin, 1999) would be a good place to start. Some months ago I was talking to Rene Padilla, one of the leading Latin American theologians. I said to him, "Rene, as I read your books, I realize that almost everything I am writing is exactly what you've been saying for twenty years. In many ways, what people are calling the emergent conversation is simply people of European descent discovering what Latin American and black and other postcolonial theologians have been saying for decades now."

Rene replied, sadly and ironically, "Yes, but remember, Latin American theology is quite rare in Latin America." Most theology there, he said, is simply exported North American theology. In other words, the thoughts and voices of the colonizers are still dominant.

I am deeply hopeful that the way forward involves a partnership between leaders like Kenzo, Padilla, and others from the global South—along with African American and indigenous North American voices and those of other minorities—joining together with those of us from the global North who do not see Western Christianity as normative. That kind of genuine partnership—not a paternalistic pseudo partnership—could be one of the most important things to happen in our lifetimes.

The work of professional philosophers and theologians like Myron Penner and Bruce Ellis Benson becomes a kind of subversive work in the academy of the West, the goal of which (I believe) is nothing short of repentance—rethinking—so that we acknowledge the ways in which our theologies have colluded with empire, colonialism, racism, consumerism, etc., through the centuries. As important as their academic work is, without voices of emerging leaders and thinkers from the global South, it will be yet another Western monotone, though.

So, my deep thanks to the organizers of this project for including Kenzo in this conversation; may that inclusion lead the way to more and more true partnership—so that voices like Kenzo's are respectfully heard by "those with ears to hear." Speaking personally, it has been deeply unsettling to begin to see the collusion of modern Western Christian theology (both Catholic and Protestant, both liberal and conservative) with colonialism and empire. But the good news of Jesus—the message of the kingdom of God, which I believe provides the only true alternative to **totalizing** (in)human empires and the metanarratives that uphold them—has never looked so good to me as it does now.

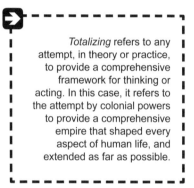

Totalizing refers to any attempt, in theory or practice, to provide a comprehensive framework for thinking or acting. In this case, it refers to the attempt by colonial powers to provide a comprehensive empire that shaped every aspect of human life, and extended as far as possible.

• DangerMouse: **Colonizing instincts alive and well**

Brian: If I follow, basically "postmodernism" is an attempt to break the hold of a philosophical superpower? To set the captives free, as it were? I could buy into that. Well, I have bought into it already, but you know what I mean.

I have to say that it, evangelicalism, does seem to be pretty much all about changing the Other to be the same as Self, motivated presumably by an insecure (and unaware) ego. The colonizing instinct is prevalent. Still. I think it is ugly.

It bothers me that our theological thinking doesn't yet have the bold language to directly challenge this tendency. We are still arguing about truth much of the time, when we should be arguing about what is sin and what is love instead. We should be figuring out how to put to death the old man rather than how to reach out to the "lost." I hate that word. It stinks of a domineering mindset.

Postcolonially yours, DangerMouse

- Jonathan Wood: **Truth affects love and sin**

DangerMouse: It seems to me that if "love" and "sin" are to be discussed, then truth has to be discussed as a sort of prolegomena. Where we fall within different conceptualizations of truth will affect how we conceptualize such truths as "love" and "sin." Do you disagree?

- DangerMouse: **Love, truth, and sin**

Jonathan, to answer your post: I have to borrow a well-known phrase and say, "That is a great question." It has revealed more of who I am to me. So thanks.

I think I do disagree. I guess I'm saying that "truth" is important. I'm saying that all these things, i.e., truth and our ideas of love and sin, are interrelated at some level. I am also saying that these ideas of what is love and what is good and bad behavior do not require an intellectual framework. I think a framework is all the poorer if it tries to exist divorced from basic emotional and behavioral reality. So, for example, if I can only define sin and love in Christian terms, I have a problem. My religious belief is divorced from everyday experienced reality and I have no way of ensuring that my framework has bearing on the real world. If I can define sin and love in terms of everyday authorities, then I can make an impact on the world around me to cause it to consider Christlike values as it goes about its daily business.

I guess my concern is that the word *religion* has roots in the concept of re-connection, but our very approach to truth is steeped in disconnection. From my perspective this seems to begin on the [wrong foot]—in this case arguing about truth largely divorced from the God-given reality we experience day to day.

So I guess I think that the conceptualization comes out of reflection on what is. Clearly there is a certain amount of the "chicken or the egg?" scenario here, but to lose connection to the reality we are trying to improve and enjoy is surely madness. I think this is the generous approach to this subject. A less generous approach would be to say it's all about the intellectual elite trying to exert control on the masses and this is merely a manifestation of the control battle between different factions in the intellectual elite. However, I'm with Napoleon when he says, "Never ascribe to malice that which can be explained by incompetence."

Acceptance and peace, DangerMouse

- Jonathan Wood: **Love and sin are not concepts**

DangerMouse: Does the way we conceptualize love and sin really matter? It seems to me that the Scriptures present us with an idea of love and sin that is in fact very concrete. Does conceiving of love and sin in Christian terms mean that we are necessarily relating abstractly to our particular place in the world today? I myself do not tend to think so.

- DangerMouse: **Love and sin are concepts**

Personally, I think it is fundamental to get these concepts right. Being aware of differences at a higher conceptual level is fun but doesn't address the issue of otherness. I think it betrays an attitude that pays lip service to valuing difference but in reality the Self still wants the Other to embrace or come over to his or her point of view.

Being able to communicate the Christian values of love and sin in the language of the Other enables us to relate to the Other in a the way that God related to us—by becoming the Other. Only going halfway in my perspective is narrow-minded and not a position of love. Attempting to use Scripture as an authority in negotiating with non-Christians

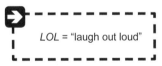

LOL = "laugh out loud"

is similar. It reminds me of the typical English response abroad—to repeat the same thing, only louder. I'm sure Monte Python covered this well. **LOL**.

Does anyone else have a view on how far we take the axe to the colonizing tree? Is it enough to chop the branches, or do we excavate the roots too? This question, I feel, is important, as it influences the whole of our stance to the non-Christian world. It impacts our understanding of the Great Commission.

Acceptance and peace, DM

- Colin Toffelmire: **Getting beyond colonization—listening to the Other**

DM: Great questions—for which I have no answers, just some thoughts and more questions. As to taking the axe to the colonial tree, beyond the question of "Should we?" stands the question of "Can we?" Is it even possible to go back and fix this mess? My guess is that it isn't. The more important question now becomes: How do we move forward? I think that Kenzo is offering us a start. Perhaps forward movement must come in the form of the colonizers sitting at the feet of their former victims and allowing themselves to hear what they believed to be their own stories retold and reinterpreted.

As to your comment about "becoming the Other," is this really possible? I thoroughly agree that we must find those places where our story intersects the story of the Other, places where we can interact and influence each-the-Other, but I can't see a scenario (apart from the incarnation itself) where we can truly become the Other. I do like the spirit behind what you're saying, though. Humility and an open heart are keys to interacting with any Other.

- DangerMouse: **Theology is not the answer**

Colin: I love the "Great questions" comment. We're all becoming little "Brians" [McLaren]. LOL.

My thought about taking the axe to the tree was an issue of heart attitude. To root out all colonial instinct. I agree with your idea of listening. Maybe as a precursor to that dialogue we could all attempt some **log-removal** ourselves. I think a lot more can be achieved in that sort of reflection than [in many other kinds of reflection].

> Here DM is alluding to Jesus' statement in the Sermon on the Mount to the effect that we must remove the beam or log from our own eye before we try to remove the splinter from our brother's or sister's eye.

The thought about "becoming the Other." Hmmm. Who knows what is possible? Does it matter? I think we've been given a beautiful example to imitate and, personally, I want to do it. To me it's not a matter of *should* or *can*. I don't really care whether I should or can. I just want to.

If I may bring a thought to the conversation, as I'm reading some of the posts I see a couple of things going on. I see that much of this conversation is about escaping the limitations of externally imposed control. The control is manifesting in the form of theology, so we are countering it. Setting the captives free, if we want to Christianize it. I see that the limited mindset is hard to escape. It appears to me that we are so used to being limited (and, as Christians, I think even more so than non-Christians) that we are uncomfortable even with the idea of being unlimited. I also see complex arguments, in our case in the form of postmodernism and subsequent theology, being set in place to excuse our emotional sense of limitation. It's like we don't like being slaves of evangelical theology, so we try to break the fetters; but we aren't used to being free men, so we look for another master to enslave us. I see this evidence in the language that we use and the attitudes we exhibit toward one another.

I also think that if the emergent church thinks that the answer lies in theology then it will fail. Don't get me wrong: I know the power of the story, and it is important to get the story right. However, the most important story is a very local story deep within our own histories and emotions, and to be honest I think there is a lack of focus by Christianity in general (including the conversation here) to tackle that local story. The big story is important, but unknown to us our unconscious stories, I think, have much more influence on our individual and collective lives. The postmodern critique gives us, in my opinion, an opportunity and an encouragement to escape the tyranny of control. Maybe we can escape the control ourselves and even give up the control of others; in this thread that would mean embracing other world perspectives in conversation.

• Whitewave: **Integrity before truth**

I'm thinkin' we can cut through some of the fog about truth or love coming first if we clear away both and say that personal honesty comes first. This will ultimately bear both truth and love as its fruit. If we keep the idea of truth as something external to us, then that is like when Jesus says, "It is not what goes into the mouth that makes you unclean . . ." A truth that belongs to another may be quite adaptable. It doesn't have to make me unclean. But if we keep the idea of truth as something that originates from inside of me, then that is like when Jesus says, "It is what comes out of the mouth that makes you unclean." That's where the "proof" is.

And what may come out is love. And it may be hate. It might be both, as the human heart is a pretty complex and messy thing. Ambivalence is our collective middle name. But all the dogmatic truths in the world that tell us to love will not be able to change the heart. In truth, we can't change at all until we've coughed up what's really in there to begin with. I like when DangerDude says, "To me it's not a matter of *should* or *can*. I don't really care whether I should or can. I just want to."

- Myron Bradley Penner: **A fully human (not just Western) Jesus**

The first time I met Kenzo he was giving a paper at the Evangelical Theological Society; and in that meeting he asked the rhetorical question, "Do I, as an African, first have to deny my African-ness—and think like a European, in Western catego-ries—before I can become a Christian?" We might continue on to ask if we must first teach indigenous peoples Plato's metaphysical fascination with the One over the Many, or Descartes' notion of the self-grounding self, before we teach them the gospel? Or is it possible that someone might encounter the grace of Jesus Christ in linguistic and cultural thoughtforms different than ones framed for us in Western

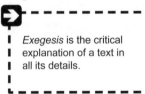

Exegesis is the critical explanation of a text in all its details.

philosophical categories and canonized in our creeds and councils? It was a wonderful thing to behold as Kenzo came to lecture on our campus to my students and showed them a picture of an "African Jesus," portrayed as a Masai chief sit-ting on a shepherd's mat. As Kenzo **exegeted** the picture for us, describing its complex relation to Christian orthodoxy and biblical categories, some of my non-Western students came alive. One, a Canadian First Nations' believer, said that this was the first time he had allowed himself to think of his cultural background as something other than a hindrance to his Christianity, and another indigenous student from the Philippines captured a vision to do theol-ogy for his people in the same manner.

What is particularly powerful about Kenzo's blog is that it highlights the fact that our Western understanding of Christianity does not exist in an historical and cultural vacuum; and yet he is appropriately cautious about elevating any cultural expression as the one in which the gospel is best communicated, whether that be modern, postmodern, or postcolonial. I am particularly struck by Kenzo's emphasis on the evangel and his point that "in postcolonial theology [evangelical theology gets] what it always wanted: . . . a

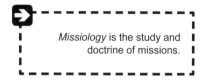

Missiology is the study and doctrine of missions.

self-theologizing church." I wonder how many of us are threatened by this notion, even while we have been giving lip service to it in our **missiologies**, because we might just have to (re)learn our theology?

Kenzo's work as a theologian is patiently teaching me that Jesus took upon himself humanity in its totality, not just *Western* humanity.

• Paula Spurr: **Heaven's glory is a multisplendored thing**

"Amen" [to Myron's post] from the back corner, said with great emphasis—or as I'm more likely to say, "Yeah, man!!"

Here is a verse that excited me so much the first time I really truly read it, from Revelation 21:24 (I'll only quote the one verse; feel free to read the rest of the chapter for context): "The nations will walk by its light, and the kings of the earth will bring their splendor into it"—talking about the New Jerusalem. Did you catch that? The kings of the earth will bring *their* splendor into it. Each king of each people will bring what is wonderful and valid from their culture and add it to the glory around the throne of God. It's a recurring thread all throughout Revelation: the love of God is for every tribe, nation, and tongue. The homogenization of the gospel so it can be spoon-fed to "heathens" makes me so sad I almost feel like puking. What have we lost? Can we regain it? I'm so glad this conversation is taking place.

- Kenzo: **Christian and postmodern**

I have been quite impressed by the exchange that this project has generated. So thank you, Myron, for the brilliant idea!

In essence, all that I could say in terms of a response to my posting has already been said more eloquently and brilliantly by others. However, I believe it still is appropriate that I add my voice to the mix to ensure that this excellent conversion remains truly postcolonial. I say "postcolonial" because one of the main worries of postcolonial theory is precisely that the subaltern may never speak! (See Gayatri Spivak's excellent essay, "Can the Subaltern Speak?" *Wedge* [Winter/Spring 1985]: 120–30.)

Before making any comment concerning the issue on hand, I believe some autobiographical info might help. Am I critical of evangelical theology and evangelical mission? Certainly. Am I opposed to evangelical theology and mission? Absolutely not! Indeed, I conscientiously and willingly sign a statement of faith that is evangelical (as defined both by my denomination and the Evangelical Theological Society—an essentially American body of scholars) every year and still see myself as postmodern! Bear with me, I will explain what I mean by "postmodern." But, first, back to my autobiography.

I was born and raised in Maduda, in the Democratic Republic of Congo (Africa). Now, Maduda is a mission station with a K–12 Christian school and a rural hospital. My grandfather was the district superintendent and both my dad and my mom worked for the school. Among our neighbors at the mission station were missionaries from Canada, the United States, Holland, and Belgium. We shared life together (sort of), and, as children, we didn't mind that our playmates had electricity and running water in their homes while we didn't. As a child I religiously attended Sunday school, even if I didn't care too much about those pictures being stuck to the flannel board. (The problem was that they kept falling down!) I grew up being that hybrid that many other Africans are: African, Christian, and Western-trained. To this day, I value all the aspects of my legacy. So, I'm critical of evangelical theology and mission, just as I'm critical of Africa, out of deep love, and nothing else.

Now, coming back to the questions that were raised in connection to my posting, I would just address a few of them. First, can anyone be an evangelical

Christian and at the same time postmodern? This question can only be answered if we define what we mean by "evangelical" and "postmodern." And that is exactly where the problem lies. At face value, it would seem easy enough to define "evangelical." Yet I've been an active member of the Evangelical Theological Society long enough to know that to define "evangelical" is easier said than done. For my part, the best I can do is to offer a confession and a testimony, as I've done above. I concede that the merit of my confession and my testimony is dependent on the trust you choose to place or not to place on the person that I am. As to the "postmodern" label, I believe we need to relax and not read too much into it. For me, postmodernism is a convenient label that stands for what David Wells calls "Our Time," that is, the current sociocultural paradigm. So, when I say I'm postmodern, I only mean that I live in a culture of postmodernity. As I understand it, postmodernism is theorized differently, depending on the individual. The result is that postmodern theories represent a spectrum with moderate postmodern theories in the middle and the most radical at both ends of the spectrum. I dare say that the situation is not different with modernity. Maybe due to my personality type and the way I have been raised, I tend to be attracted by the middle ground. So even when I read Derrida, Foucault, Lyotard, or Deleuze and Guattari, I always try my best to keep those insights that are most likely to be constructive to my African Christian identity. By the way, it is only arrogance that leads François Lyotard to say that postmodernity is "the condition of knowledge in the most highly developed [read Western] societies" (François Lyotard, *The Postmodern Condition* [Minneapolis: University of Minnesota Press, 1984], xxiii). As I have argued elsewhere, what is nowadays being acclaimed as postmodern is consonant with traditional African **episteme**. (There we go again, one of those words—unfortunately, I have no dynamic equivalent in my repertoire!) See, for instance, Mabiala Justin-Robert Kenzo, "Thinking Otherwise About Africa: Postcolonialism, Postmodernism, and the Future of African Theology," *Exchange* 31/4 (2002): 323–41.

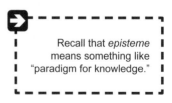

Recall that *episteme* means something like "paradigm for knowledge."

So back to the question: Can anyone be an evangelical Christian and at the same time postmodern? Honestly, I would hope so. Lamin Sanneh has argued forcefully that one of the defining characteristics of Christianity is translatability. (Aha, this time it is not my word!) In other words, unlike Islam, for instance,

Christianity is translatable. It knows how to speak into new cultural situations. As far as I know, no one chooses his or her culture. We're all born into one. If postmodernity defines the culture of our time, the best we can do is to engage it. That is, we need to ask ourselves how best we can honor the Lord as his witnesses here and now.

Second, let me say something about the complaint concerning language and the use of words. [Edited out of the book were some posts that commented very negatively on Kenzo's use of technical vocabulary, which was difficult for some to follow.] It is quite interesting that the concern in our ongoing exchange has been about how we should simplify "our" language and use "common words" which do not require one to check the dictionary (English dictionary, of course). I giggle because this point brilliantly illustrates what I hope evangelical theology would not become: speaking only from one perspective with little concern for the Other. In fact, while you're concerned about using a more accessible language, my concern has been finding words (yes, finding them from the dictionary) that hopefully would make sense to you while at the same time communicating my thoughts. Do you realize that no matter how supposedly simple your own language is, I have to use a dictionary to check some of your words? Ah, if only you knew how frustrating it can be to express oneself in one of the most confusing languages that ever existed! It took me forever to get my "blog" ready, it is taking me forever to get this long response ready, and so on, because **I didn't speak English until I was twenty-five** (a slow learner, indeed!). Don't get me wrong; I'm not whining. It has been my life at the margins, at the border. It is the in-between life of a hybrid.

> The editors would like to note that English is Kenzo's *fifth* language.

My appeal to the Anglo-American evangelical church is for more sensitivity toward the evangelical church in the global South. I believe it was the former Canadian prime minister, Pierre Elliot Trudeau, who once said in reference to the United States: "Living next to you is in some ways like sleeping with an elephant. No matter how friendly and even-tempered is the beast, if I can call it that, one is affected by every twitch and grunt." Now I have no idea what the politics behind the statement were, but it makes a relevant point.

Third, [Brian and some postmodern evangelicals may be frightened by Western symbols and their colonizing effect on our theology, and therefore desire to deconstruct them. However, s]ome of the African images of Christ scare me too. It is not just Western theological constructs that stand in need of deconstruction (yes, there can be no reformation without deconstruction). African theological constructs also stand in need of deconstruction. Thank God, the legitimate effort on the part of Africans to give the Christ in whom they have believed an African name has generated a lively debate. My hope is that Westerners would pay attention to what is happening theologically in Africa and contribute to the debate that is taking place on the continent as Africans seek to translate their faith into a vernacular language. As Andrew Walls has been arguing, what is happening in Africa today is very similar to what happened in the West between the second and fifth century AD. Christianity has entered a new culture and is in a quest for an appropriate language. That Africans are using African images, symbols, and metaphors to express the mystery of our faith is quite legitimate. However, some of these images, symbols, and metaphors need to be redefined to better express the mystery of the Christian faith. An example is given by **the Nicene fathers**. To express the mystery of Christ, they chose Greek words and concepts. However, they took care to redefine some of these. For instance, to avoid the natural association between *generation* and *creation*, they made it clear that in the case of Jesus generation did not mean creation. Hence they say about Jesus that he is 1) "the only-begotten Son of God"; 2) "begotten of the Father before all worlds"; 3) "God of God, Light of Light"; 4) "very God of very God"; 5) "begotten, not made"; 6) "being of one substance (***homoousion***) with the Father." Here we have an excellent example of contextualization.

The *Nicene fathers* were the Christian thinkers who helped frame the Nicene Creed at the Council of Nicaea in 325 AD, which is the basis for Christian orthodoxy still today.

Homoousion in Greek literally means "of same substance." It is used in relation to Jesus to indicate that Jesus is the same as God the Father.

- Colin Toffelmire: **Who may do postcolonial theology?**

Kenzo: First of all I must say that it's great to hear your thoughts on this stuff—which is actually related to the question I have concerning postcolonial theology and interpretation. Simply put, is it possible for me, as a (very) white Canadian evangelical, to engage in postcolonial interpretation, or is this simply a task better left to "hybrids" (by which I assume you mean people whose development has been shaped by multiple cultures/heritages) such as yourself?

- Paula: **It's not about us**

Kenzo: Thank you so much for your latest post! I wanted to thank you specifically for two things: 1) For quoting my former prime minister, P. E. Trudeau! That is one of my favorite quotes, and I love that you use it in this setting! You have brought a smile to my face. 2) For reminding all of us, me especially, that we are not the only people on this planet (talk about self-centered). Really, I don't know why the rest of the world puts up with North America at *all*! Thank you for adding your voice to this conversation; thank you for sitting beside your dictionary and carefully choosing the proper words; and thank you, thank you, thank you for your humility. It is an example to me that I will not soon forget.

- Kenzo: **Postcolonial theology may be done by anyone with the Spirit**

Colin: I believe that postcolonialism is more a question of attitude than geography. To a degree, we've all been impacted by colonialism. The irony with colonialism is that once the West invented "the Orient" or "African" as the Other of the Westerner, the West became dependent on this Other for its survival. Now, I'm not here talking about economic survival (although there was a great deal of that too) but of survival of the conscious self. The Western self became prisoner of the modern binary opposition: the Westerner is defined as white, rational, civilized, over against the Other who is black (or simply nonwhite), superstitious, and uncivilized. We all need to learn to live after the colony; that is, with no metropolitan center. This translates into theology as resistance toward the temptation of self-centeredness (Don't we struggle with that one?) and learning to love the Other as oneself and finding God in unexpected places. The latter is not just a sign of political correctness, but an expression of a profound belief that God, through the Holy Spirit, is at work here and now in the borderlands and margins of our own society.

- Moose Lips: **Need for Holy Spirit**

    I am unfamiliar with this form of language, so you will have to forgive me if what I say doesn't make sense, but could I suggest a clarification of the term "interpretation"? I appreciated Kenzo's response because he essentially nailed it down as being the work of the Holy Spirit that allows for this engagement to occur and cross these boundaries. Though I think a real fulfillment of this can occur only through the Holy Spirit, I would also suggest that this is limited in our time and that we must look to that eschatological statement that "one day every knee will bow and every tongue confess"; and in the meantime we must not only be denying ourselves but replacing ourselves and becoming **Christocentric**. I would suggest that this really allows only for a limited postcolonial interpretation for now.

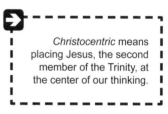

Christocentric means placing Jesus, the second member of the Trinity, at the center of our thinking.

POSTMODERN APOLOGETICS

Myron Bradley Penner

Modernity is often labeled as the age of science, or as the age of reason, but I would like to add one more moniker: modernity is also the age of apologetics. In modernity, traditional forms of authority (viz. church and state) are rejected and human reason is reimagined as universal and objective so that it can fill the authority vacuum. In other words, it is to *reason* (as universal and objective) that one must look in modernity for the authority and legitimacy of one's beliefs and actions. (And one must do it for oneself!) What is more, moderns understand the "universal" and "objective" dimensions of human reason in terms of the modern ideals of secularism (religious neutrality), democracy (rule by the majority), science (empiricism), and disinterestedness (unbiased opinion).

Science, understood (roughly) as the free and disinterested attempt to unify the various dimensions of human sense experience under a common theory, became the paradigm of rational inquiry—for philosophy as well as natural science. Subsequently, modernism challenges the very source and basis of Christian belief—for Christianity could hitherto claim very little by way of these modern ideals. It is little wonder, then, that Christians found it necessary to take up the arms of modern rationality and defend themselves. In short, in response to the attacks on Christian belief from modern philosophy, modern evangelical Christians developed a "scientific" apologetic, modeled after the philosophical method and rigor of modern **analytic philosophy**, which attempted to establish the universal rationality of Christian belief using the same "objective" and "presupposition-less" premises required by modern empirical science.

> Analytic philosophy refers to the method of doing philosophy (predominantly in Britain and North America) that takes the logical analysis of concepts as the proper task of philosophy.
>
> Kerygma is the Greek word used in the New Testament to refer to the proclamation of the gospel.

My suggestion is that, in light of postmodern critiques of modernity, evangelicals should adopt a form of apologetic that is *kerygmatic* in nature, rather than a modern "scientific" apologetic. Perhaps the model for the Christian thinker can be someone other than an analytic philosopher.

But what sort of model should we have for apologetics—"the rational defense of the faith"—other than the analytic philosopher, with her emphasis on demonstrating or proving that the propositions of Christianity are both universally and objectively true? Make no mistake, I greatly value the insights of analytic philosophy and admire its rigor; but perhaps we should consider the New Testament apostle (or Old Testament prophet) as an alternate model for our apologetic efforts.[1] St. Paul never tires of pointing out that apostles and prophets, unlike modern philosophers, do not predicate their authority on clever arguments, logical coherence, rhetorical brilliance, or anything like the modern conception of human reason, but on the divine source of their message. It is not so much that the apostle cannot or even will not engage in rhetorical brilliance or philosophical and logical argumentation—as Paul is certainly capable and often does; it is rather that the apostle does not base the *authority* of his or her message on his or her own intellectual resources. The apostle's primary mode of address, then, is kerygma, proclamation or preaching, and any argumentation is a secondary discourse designed to facilitate the primary one.

There are a number of reasons why we might want to consider the apostle as the exemplar for a new kind of apologetics. To begin with, the modern paradigm of empirical science does not accord well with the biblical portrayal of Christianity. Modern science—to be distinguished from the premodern paradigm of *natural* science—models the universe as brute and irrational and sees its task as directing the powers of human reason (conceived in the terms described above) toward the mastery of its object, having begged no questions with regard to its theoretical status. **Søren Kierkegaard** is perhaps the first modern thinker to perceive the deep-seated disparity between the modern scientific paradigm and biblical Christianity; and he subsequently argues vigorously that Christianity cannot be assimilated to modern science and philosophy, as modern apologists wish.

Søren Kierkegaard was a mid-nineteenth-century Danish philosopher and theologian who is widely (but not entirely correctly) known as the father of existentialism because of his emphasis on subjectivity and individual responsibility.

From the Christian point of view, the truth about Christianity cannot be found in modern-styled objectivity.[2] Not only does the essence of Christianity concern the desperate need of humans and God's gracious (and personal) response to our need, but it also starts with the assumption that human being (even with human reason) is unable to save itself. Christian truth presumes to *master us*, rather than to be *mastered by us*. Therefore, whenever I try to establish the fundamental reasonability of Christianity in modern terms, I remove its fundamental "offense" to reason and transform Christianity into something domestic, with nothing other than a cognitive claim on my life. Christianity, however, is a *way of being*, or what Kierkegaard calls an "actuality"—a way of living with and before God—and not just a cognitive event involving intellectual assent to a set of propositions. It involves the acts of God himself in response to our condition as sinful persons and requires our being saved from this condition of brokenness and sinfulness through a total response that can only be described in theological categories like sin, repentance, and salvation that necessarily relate to the subjectivity of human beings. These personal categories cannot be assimilated into the objective discourse of modern science and point to subjective realities that are more appropriately dealt with in sermons.

I also want briefly to mention one other important problem with using modern (objective and universal) apologetic arguments to defend Christianity, though there are others as well. Modern objectivity refuses to acknowledge the ethical dimensions of arguments, and treats them abstractly and acontextually, and ignores the personal and social dimension of reason. The trouble, of course, is that arguments *always* are situated and made by persons, and as such are ethical entities. Adopting a modern paradigm predisposes apologists to ignore that, first, arguments, like words, are more than just formal operations that yield true conclusions. Arguments never mean anything until they are used by persons in a social context to *do* something, and one may use a perfectly valid argument with all true premises to do something unethical (like, for example, belittle or domineer someone). A modern, objective approach to apologetic arguments also inclines Christian apologists to overlook the fact that their arguments may be used to support an oppressive and socially unjust form of Christianity, and therefore to that degree fail to justify *actual* Christianity.

But what if we modeled our apologetic heroes after apostles and not analytic philosophers? What if we made love, and not modern rationality, the hallmark of our defense of Christianity, and took kerygma, not logic, as the form of our apologetic discourse?

The sort of kerygmatic apologetics I mean to endorse is one that takes lightly neither issues of truth nor the rationality of Christian belief. Biblically, the basis for and motivation of kerygma is love, and this means that at the core of a kerygmatic apologetic will be a love-centered rationality. The irony of Christian love is that it is characterized by self-donation; it gives itself up to find itself. A love-centered rationality will have as its character an appropriate *humility*, a personal and social *situatedness* that takes human embodiment seriously (i.e., it is not a disembodied rationality) within an overarching gospel narrative, and, above all, is characterized by an *interest* in the welfare and perspective of others. Postmodern evangelicals, however, do not thereby relinquish the pursuit of the good, the true, and the beautiful, nor do they require their interlocutors (i.e., their *neighbors*) to either. My construal of postmodernity calls us into even more serious and patient, rational dialogue with those with whom we disagree about the most important things than does modernity, for it calls us to the **dialectical** task of recognizing alternate points of view and carefully establishing our Christian convictions in dialogue with them. There is, if you will, what we might call after Kierkegaard a "logic of insanity"[3] that argues for the **Socratic** affirmation of "the superiority of heaven-sent madness over man-made sanity."[4]

> *Dialectical* here refers to the sort of back-and-forth reasoning that happens in conversation or when one thinks through both sides of an argument.
>
> *Socratic* is a reference to the ancient Greek philosopher Socrates (470–399 BC).

The type of postmodern kerygmatic apologetic I envision will have several identifiable aspects. First, it will be *occasional*, not systematic or "universal." The communication of God's truth is not something the apostle presents as a scientific theory that is able to answer a set of theoretical questions. A kerygmatic apologetic will subsequently involve a particular person addressing a specific audience that has a concrete set of concerns about life, God, and the world. It will not deal in hypothetical questions or answers that do not arise from the context of the audience's lives and does not propose to offer answers that have not been personally won in the circumstances of the Christian's own life.

Second, a kerygmatic apologetic will be *confessional*. Its primary mode of discourse will be in the category of *witness*. An apostle does not present her message in the form of objective and universal truths, but as a confession of or witness to a personal word she has received from God. A witness, then, is someone who confesses her convictions within the wider context of her life and therefore displays an existentially embodied argument. (And in the wider context of the church, the Christian witness becomes a *socially* embodied argument.) The act of confession or witness subverts the modern subject-object split and provides the starting point for genuine dialogue and effective apologetic argument by honestly confessing one's convictions and offering a starting point for dialogue. Witness is, in other words, what Stan Hauerwas calls "the condition necessary to begin argument."[5] Witness doesn't *end* arguments, but it determines the kind and shape that our arguments and apologetic dialogues will take. Witness creates the conditions for the intelligibility of the gospel insofar as it demonstrates a way of being in which its claims make sense.

Occasional is used here to indicate that apologetics should focus on specific questions or challenges to Christian faith that arise in specific life contexts, rather than formulating universal systems of thought.

Confessional here means confessing a creed or acknowledging a set of beliefs, not confessing sin.

Eschatological here refers to the Greek word *eschaton*, which means "the end or culmination of history."

Penultimate literally means "next to last"; here it refers more to something that is less than ultimate.

Third, such an apologetic will also have an *eschatological* character that acknowledges its conclusions as finite, fallible, and **penultimate**. The arguments and propositions of the apologetic witness will anticipate the new order inaugurated by the return of Jesus Christ and the full presence of God, in which the truth is fully and finally revealed. As a result, the sort of reasoning of the apostle is from within a kind of **meganarrative** that is a particular community's story of the world (with global implications), as opposed to the **metanarrative** of modernity, which purports to tell everyone's presuppositionless story of the world.[6]

> **Meganarrative** means "big story" and is used to refer to a story or worldview that attempts to provide a comprehensive account of reality.
>
> **Metanarrative** is a story or account of everything that claims to be self-evident. See Blog 1 for more.

Fourth, and finally, a postmodern kerygmatic apologetic is one that addresses the whole person; that is, it is *holistic*. Logical argumentation is one dimension of defending Christian faith, but insofar as it is gospel, Christianity addresses the whole person and is concerned with issues of social justice as well as propositional or logical correctness. The goal, furthermore, is not one of rational domination but of "winning" the person over. Kierkegaard summarizes the situation nicely:

> Long, long before the enemy thinks of seeking agreement, the loving one is already in agreement with him; and not only that, no, he has gone over to the enemy's side, is fighting for his cause. . . . See, this can be called a battle of love or a battle in love! To fight with the help of the good *against* the enemy—that is laudable and noble; but to fight *for* the enemy—and against whom? Against oneself, if you will—this, yes, this is loving, or this is the conciliatory spirit in love.[7]

COMMENTS

THREAD ONE:
Subjective Apologetics

- AI: **Can we practice postmodern apologetics?**

Can anyone help me from a . . . postmodern evangelical perspective to address the following three current apologetic issues?

1. The **Jesus Seminar** and Dan Brown's *DaVinci Code*. Both of these have captured the allegiance of millions of enthusiasts in our midst who are fleeing from Christian communities with their very unorthodox view of Jesus, including my niece and nephew.

2. The naturalist[ic] materialism that has such a firm grip on our educational and scientific establishments that they seem to be utterly unwilling to consider any evidence that suggests intelligent design in the cosmos and the biosphere.

     The Jesus Seminar is a twice-a-year meeting of a group of New Testament scholars dedicated to studying the historicity of Jesus from a religiously neutral framework. The result of their work is largely at odds with traditional (conservative) claims about Jesus.

3. The antiheterosexist crusade that seeks to ban from public education, media, government, and anywhere in the public square all expressions of preference for heterosexual marriage. My grandkids are being taught this in books and class in public school.

How do . . . postmodern evangelical perspectives address these current issues in our midst? Shalom, Al

- Bob Robinson: **An *"Emmanuel* apologetic" and distinguishing between primary and secondary levels of discourse**

Al: The issue with many Christians sympathetic to postmodernism is less with whether or not propositional truth exists than with how much authority we will place in *our articulation* of such propositional truth. Propositions are man-made statements created *from* the "Truth" that is *God and his story revealed to us.* We arrive at a proposition via interaction with **Emmanuel.** But since our propositions are *man-made linguistic articulations* of what we believe God is saying to us, we must hold these propositions loosely.

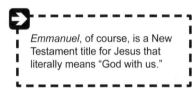

Emmanuel, of course, is a New Testament title for Jesus that literally means "God with us."

Lifting up truth claims in the modern world is troublesome in that we've been taught in modernity that in order for something to be "true" it must stand up to the legitimating process of "objective reason." But a postmodern refutes this: "Wait a minute! Objective reason is not the ultimate legitimator of truth! Any claim of knowing absolute truth through 'objective reason' is really a word game that covers up some subjective point of view."

So . . . my [basic] premise [is]: "Truth" must be *incarnational* truth—the "God with us" of an Emmanuel apologetic. Any proposition we articulate flows from that, not the other way around. As Myron Penner writes, "An apostle does not present her message in the form of objective and universal truths, but as a confession of or witness to a personal word she has received from God."

As for your worries [reflected in an earlier post] that I am, as a commenter (or Penner or any of the other main contributors to this [book are]), attempting to create "either/or/only" arguments, I just don't see it. In rhetorical style, we naturally must draw contrasts to make our points, and readers must allow for that. I see that Penner himself wrote in this post, "The apostle's *primary* mode of address, then, is kerygma, proclamation or preaching, and any argumentation is a *secondary* discourse designed to facilitate the primary one" (emphasis mine). This is not an "either/or/only" argument but an appeal to a hierarchy of discourse—a primary and then a secondary one.

So to answer your questions, we should follow Myron's primary/secondary course. To the Jesus Seminar and *DaVinci Code* apologists, I'd say that of course there are reasoned arguments that clearly refute them. But our intellectual and reasoned arguments mean little to nothing if we are not displaying the true Jesus before them as a community of believers. To merely have "better arguments" reduces the situation to bantering and who has better debating skills. But to have a kerygma that projects "This is the real Christ—compassion and love and a resurrection life filled with hope" gives credence to our reasoned statements that simply cannot be argued with. I submit that the reason [**John Dominic**] **Crossan** and Brown get a hearing is because the Christian community has done such a poor job of being Emmanuel in this world. The plausibility of their counter to Christianity exists *because* the Christian "God with us" witness has been so implausible (it has been so poorly lived out).

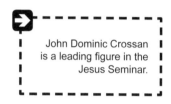

John Dominic Crossan is a leading figure in the Jesus Seminar.

To the naturalist/materialist who cannot accept an intelligent designer, we simply dismiss them as too modern and unable to accept the mysterious and supernatural. Modern Darwinist theory will die under the weight of postmodernity, since it is so dependent on naturalist/materialist causes. Darwinism is the epitome of modern thought—the idea that we can arrive at "truth" through objective science. It does not allow for a "subject" to exist that cannot be examined objectively; that is, a Creator who made the world out of his love. This "Truth" cannot be found through objective science *alone*; it is found in the story he reveals to us (both in the Scriptures and in the very creation we study). When we counter with nothing more than another scientific debate, appealing to "reason" instead of the wonder of the story, then it again is reduced to bantering and who has better debating skills. Not that we cannot appeal to the wonder of the design in creation, but that cannot be the primary apologetic; it is the secondary apologetic.

To the "antiheterosexist crusaders," we must live out a loving marital heterosexual life that shows that traditional marriage models true love more than any other kind of "love" that people presume exists. Any other argument without that primary proclamation sounds hollow. By the way, we evangelicals have done a *very poor* job of doing this, since our divorce rate is as high, if not higher, than that of the general public. No wonder people scoff at our attempts to tell them that God's preference is heterosexuality, since we have not portrayed a very good Emmanuel apologetic in that regard!

- Jonathan M: **Kierkegaard and postmodernism**

[Myron:] Thank you for a very good article on "apologetics." I was a bit skeptical at first, knowing that you used Kierkegaard and Kierkegaard expressly thought Christianity hardly needed a "defense."

Anyway, I do take issue with one part of your thinking. It is often assumed that modernism began around the time of Descartes and company. It does depend on what we mean by "modernism," of course. But taking the way you define "modernism," it is clear that one could date modernism to begin at **scholasticism** in the twelfth century, with Aquinas and company being the apologists for an objective reason-based faith. If you read any of Harold Berman's work on this, it is clear that the scientific paradigm really began with theological—not secular—thought, beginning in the eleventh/twelfth century.

> *Scholasticism* refers to the development of systematic theological and philosophical perspectives in medieval times, through the use of logic and a recovery of classical Greek philosophy.
>
> Erasmus of Rotterdam was a late-fifteenth-century to early-sixteenth-century Dutch philosopher and theologian.

That said, I note with interest that you say that "Søren Kierkegaard is perhaps the first modern thinker to perceive the deep-seated disparity between the modern scientific paradigm and biblical Christianity; and he subsequently argues vigorously that Christianity cannot be assimilated to modern science and philosophy, as modern apologists wish."

I would agree with this statement except for the word *first*: for **Erasmus of Rotterdam** is probably one of the best-known examples of arguing against scholastic certainty and apologetics. In a sense, I think most Christians who are knowledgeable about history overlook him being the first "postmodern" Christian thinker. I mean, how many Christians before Erasmus can claim to say "Whether [a tenet of faith] is true or not, I do not know; I am satisfied that it is not heretical"?

How about a little more Erasmus of Rotterdam recognition?

- Myron Bradley Penner: **Kierkegaard and defining modernity**

Thank you for your engaging response and comments, Jonathan M. First, I must confess a minimal competence in medieval philosophy and theology as a whole, and thus my failure to deal much with Erasmus of Rotterdam is due in large part to my ignorance. However, there are some other reasons why it might not be necessary for me to cite Erasmus. As a matter of fact, I mention Kierkegaard as the first thinker to perceive the disparity between *modern* science and Christianity. It would be anachronistic to attribute such a position to Erasmus, as he is (in my view) not dealing with modern science, however critical he is of scholasticism and however much the seeds of modern empiricism derive from aspects of the medieval thought of which Erasmus is aware. There is a definite shift that happens in (or perhaps, "is ratified in" is a better locution) modernity—and Descartes is *representative* of that shift. I point to him as the progenitor of modernity, as do many others, because he lays it all out so nicely and clearly for us, not because he is entirely original. Of course the modern developments in philosophy are built upon previous thinking, just as Einstein's discovery of relativity in physics, which led us to reconceive the physical nature of the universe, was built on prior scientific developments.

What needs to be kept clear, here, is my claim that there is a different conception of both reason and science that emerges in modernity—one that reconceives reason according to a procedural and formal logic, as opposed to a premodern logos with its shared structure between mind and cosmos. This view of reason is inconceivable to Thomas, Anselm, Augustine, or the apostles Paul and John. I have already argued this in more detail in my "Christianity and the Postmodern Turn: Some Preliminary Considerations," in *Christianity and the Postmodern Turn: Six Views*, Myron B. Penner, editor (Grand Rapids: Brazos, 2005), 13–34.

THREAD TWO:
MODERN VS. POSTMODERN APOLOGETICS

- Scott Pruett: **Postmodernism's false dichotomies**

While [Penner's] article offers some valid critiques of modernity, I think it does not affirm what is, in fact, biblical underlying certain ideas that have been abused by secular modernists. Many authors have offered similar critiques of modernity and classical apologetics without seeing the need or prudence of questioning its very foundations. I think that Penner's conclusions rest on a number of false dichotomies.

1. Modernity vs. postmodernity

Penner seems to be suggesting that thinking objectively and rationally means thinking without bias and presuppositions. I believe there is some equivocation on the word *objective* here. There is a difference between thinking that there is objective truth and thinking that you know it objectively (i.e., without bias or error). Postmoderns are right to question presuppositions and **human fallibility**, but we lose all tools of discourse if we go beyond this to conclude that no one, then, has any better reasoned belief than another or that truth itself is a vapor. It does seem warranted to conclude that we ought to be humble regarding our fallibility, more introspective in our suppositions, and more rigorous in our application of reason. Penner says he "greatly values the insights of analytic philosophy and admires its rigor." But if these things get us nowhere, then what is there to value? And if they do have merit, then let's use them to their fullest advantage.

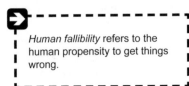

Human fallibility refers to the human propensity to get things wrong.

2. Authority of revelation vs. reason

The problem with secular modernists was that they did not accept revelation at all. But Christian "modernists" accept it as objective truth and apply it as the foundation, frame, and fence for rational discourse. St. Paul rightly warns against vain philosophy according to human tradition, but when philosophy is grounded in those truths revealed by the Author of reason, then we are privileged to taste the "mind of Christ." And if we reject reason in relation to revelation, then the very words of God become nothing but unprocessed photons striking the retina.

3. Science vs. Christianity

There seems to be a driving need to segregate the world of empirical science from the world of "faith." I think this is a response to the imagined hostility of the one to the other. However, we are now living in an age where we have the best scientific reasons ever to believe in a loving and intimate Creator. The problem is not that there is no good reason to believe that science is opposed to the God of the Bible; [instead] the problem is that science has been secularized and its very definition has been changed to exclude the supernatural from consideration. Secular scientists are now more concerned with getting a certain kind of answer than with getting the right answer. The field of science has a deeply Christian legacy, and there has been a recent resurgence in Christian scholarship. There is no sense in abandoning a healthy ship.

4. Kerygmatic vs. rational and objective approaches (or cognitive claims vs. subjective "actuality")

But is the "kerygma" which we should share grounded in truth? When we tell our story is it an objectively true story, and if not, why is there any reason or passion for sharing it? If it is not based on objective truth, then we are simply peddling an interesting story and we are ascribing a mystical value to it that has no more weight than a Dr. Phil book. Our story can be both true in the objective sense and efficacious in a subjective sense. Indeed, it has "actuality" because of the power in the truth that it contains. And when we tell that story, we are offering a series of cognitive claims. Even if a story were metaphor (like the parables), the very meaning of those metaphors is a matter of rational proposition.

5. Arguments and reason vs. love and empathy

To say that our beliefs are objectively true and advocating for them is not to say that you cannot give personal expression to these truths. In fact, those truths are the very things that impel us to love our neighbors (and enemies) and to meet them at the point of their need. How would we know how we ought to love them if not for the very things which apologists seek to defend, since one man's love (according to his own fancies) is another man's coddling?

It is true that you may win an argument but lose a soul, but every good apologist should know this. And for those who don't, the answer is not to surrender our claims to truth and the reasons for them; the answer is to refine our tactics, character, and wisdom. As St. Peter says, we should be ready to give a defense, but we should do this with gentleness and respect. And we should know when a good intellectual response is called for and when an outstretched hand and a willing ear are in order.

- Kerby Redekop: **Postmodernism recontextualizes, not dichotomizes**

Mr. Pruett: Thanks for a different perspective on this topic. You are certainly right to say that there are some "good, beautiful, and true" foundations to modernity (to quote Penner's article) as well as to postmodernity and we would do well to recognize them. Things such as individualism (a personal faith) and technology (medical, especially) were devised through modernity and have become important aspects of the redemption of creation. I think the point that Myron is making (he surely recognizes these aspects to modernity) is that anything can be taken to extremes and it is up to us to remedy the extremes which modernity has been taken to. I don't see him advocating a rejection of the good aspects of modernity—he is simply trying to retain them but place them in a different framework which will help us to avoid making the same errors again. This is what I believe postmodernity is all about.

You point out some "false dichotomies" and you are certainly right. There is no disjunction between reason/revelation, science/Christianity, etc. However, the relationship between these pairs is not patently obvious. Modernity was the age in which faith and reason became opposed.

I see Myron taking things like science, reason, objectivity, and arguments and placing them into a context different from the modern context which caused these things to become skewed in so much Christian and secular thinking. By placing science within the realm of faith, science is allowed to aid faith, something which modernity did not allow. Furthermore, notice that science is less important than faith—it is only penultimate, to use another word of Penner's.

Likewise, arguments/reason/rationality/objectivity are all important aspects of modernity which Penner goes to pains to point out that he values and does not reject. However, he wishes to make these concepts penultimate to faith. In this way love and subjectivity come to govern our use of arguments/reason, etc. So, in Penner's interpretation of postmodernity, the good things of modernity are affirmed, but placed within a different framework that holds them in a proper tension with other key Christian concepts which modernity de-emphasized.

So I would say that on my interpretation of this article your false dichotomies are in themselves an incorrect interpretation of Penner's article. Read carefully, I think he can be understood as affirming those things about which you are concerned to retain, while not allowing them to become more important than they really are to a true Christian faith.

Seeking understanding, Kerby

• Myron Bradley Penner: **Authority, revelation, and more**

Thanks, Scott, for taking the time to voice your concerns about my take on postmodern apologetics. I think Kirby has drafted a reply that is substantially how I see things, but let me add a few comments:

First, I am not sure I sufficiently communicated to you that what I oppose is *modern* objectivity—which I take to be a unique critter in the history of human ideas, although not completely differentiated from its premodern or postmodern forms. I am not against "objectivity" in the sense that we are referring to something that exists the way it is independently of its perceivers. In the end, if this point is not sufficiently appreciated it will lead one to inadequate interpretations of me.

Regarding false dichotomy #1, "modernity vs. postmodernity": I trust I do not "seem to be suggesting that thinking objectively and rationally means thinking without bias and presuppositions." What I mean to suggest instead is that this is how modernity thinks about objectivity (as an ideal) and that sort of objectivity is a **chimera**. And I certainly meant it when I said that I value the insights and rigor of analytic philosophy and therefore did not, as you claim, state that "these things get us nowhere." They *do* get us somewhere, just not where many analytic philosophers think they do. The insights of analytic philosophy offer rigorous analyses of our concepts that we employ in our philosophical discourse and check them for coherence and logical extension.

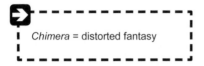

Chimera = distorted fantasy

Regarding false dichotomy #2, "authority of revelation vs. reason": To begin with, nowhere have I knowingly juxtaposed faith (or revelation) and reason. I have tried to advocate for a transformation of the categories in which we understand how reason and revelation work together. I quite like your analogy from photoreception to the reception of God's revelation. But it seems to play much better in my postmodern schema than a modern one. You see, what I take your analogy about photoreception to indicate is that just as the mere retinal bombardment by photons does not amount to perception, so too the mere fact of God's giving us a revelation does not guarantee our reception of it as revelation. In other words, it appears that your analogy supports my claim that the "absolute truths" of God's revelation are not rationally compelling in the universal and objective reason of modernity, rather than detracts from it. It takes something else—what modernity would call an appeal to subjectivity—to recognize and accept God's revelation as such, namely faith and repentance. That cannot be assimilated, I claim, into an objective scientific discourse (in the modern sense of science and objectivity). Please note, as well, that my contention above regarding the authority of revelation is that modern apologists who attempt to establish the authority of revelation according to the standards of modern criteria for rationality implicitly deny the apostolic source of authority, which was always and only God's revelation to them (cf. 1 Corinthians 1:18–2:16).

One last thing on authority and revelation, whenever St. Paul and the other apostles appeal to the fact of the resurrection, it is quite a different thing than the modern apologist's attempt to prove the resurrection using modern apologetic arguments. There is a vast difference in claiming something is true and claiming to be able to prove it. The only "proofs" of resurrection ever offered in the New

Testament is witness. This distinction between proof and claims to truth is an essential one to the logic of my blog.

Regarding false dichotomy #3, "science vs. Christianity": Again, nowhere do I intend to impugn "science" in the broadest sense of the term (i.e., the ordered knowledge of the sensible, material world), but rather hope to have made it clear that what I am lampooning is modern science, which is *empirical* science. This is to be distinguished from the natural science of Aristotle, Aquinas, and just premodernity in general. Modern science, after Bacon, purports to beg no questions and it is this which Lyotard identifies as providing modernity with its self-legitimating "metanarrative." It is this view of science that I place at odds with Christianity, not science ***simpliciter***. And note that much of what goes on in modern empirical science will be perfectly amenable to my position insofar as it does not depend upon or follow from its methodological presuppositions. It is not empirical experience I am after, but a certain theory of it.

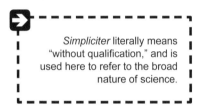

Simpliciter literally means "without qualification," and is used here to refer to the broad nature of science.

Regarding false dichotomy #4, "kerygmatic vs. rational and objective approaches": Please note my prefatory comments regarding objectivity. And of course kerygma is grounded in the truth—did I not say as much? Did I not ground the authority of Christian truth claims in their divine source? But again, as noted above, there is a vast difference between something's being true and our being able to prove it as such. Modern emphases on absolute truth and objectivity entail that the truth, if it is to be accepted as such, will always be (at least in principle) demonstrable according to the canons of modern rationality. I am contesting that, but not our ability to reason nor truth itself.

Regarding false dichotomy #5, "arguments and reason vs. love and empathy": I am not sure what to say at this point, because I have tried to make it clear, both in this response and the blog itself, that I do not juxtapose love and reason, empathy or argument, etc. As a matter of fact, in the blog itself I advocate a "love-centered rationality"!

Thanks again for giving me the opportunity to clarify my thoughts. I hope this has done so.

- AI: **Paul is not a postmodernist**

A. General comments

Thanks, Scott, for elucidating many of Myron Penner's false dichotomies. I support your contentions heartily.

Thanks, Myron, for letting us read your proposals for postmodern "kerygmatic" apologetics prior to their publication. . . . You clearly touch on many points to which I and other evangelicals could voice a hearty "Amen!" Love as a motive for all ministries expressed in both words and deeds is a given, not in dispute by any evangelicals in our time (as far as I know), though hate has been voiced by some of the revered church fathers, particularly as addressed to Jews. The need to experience personally the gospel truth we proclaim is another motherhood issue.

The above are affirmed by Kierkegaard and Westphal, and hence they too must be affirmed in so doing. However, in my humble opinion there are many dimensions to Kierkegaard and Westphal that should not be so easily baptized into contemporary evangelicalism. For example, Kierkegaard's whole "Truth is subjectivity" theme (which you already affirmed in an earlier response) can likely lead to chaos in Christian ministry. Sadly, Kierkegaard alleges the spiritual superiority of the heathen who bows in utterly sincere prayer to an idol he has just fashioned over the "dead orthodox" Christian clergy and laity of Copenhagen who believe the Apostles' Creed and the Bible but whom Kierkegaard faults for other real and/or imagined shortcomings. This perspective prompted **Jean Paul Sartre** to claim Kierkegaard as the "father of existentialism." Kierkegaard thus inspired Sartre's leadership as the last century's most influential atheist. How dare evangelicals follow Kierkegaard uncritically here? Have you read or learned from D. A. Carson's critique of Westphal's postmodernism (see D. A. Carson, "Maintaining Scientific and Christian Truths in a Postmodern World," *Science & Christian Belief* 14, no. 2, [October 2002]: 107–22)?

> → Jean Paul Sartre was a mid-twentieth-century French existentialist philosopher.
>
> *JW* here undoubtedly is a reference to Jehovah's Witnesses.

It seems to me, Myron, that most of your essay could be rewritten by a **JW**, Mormon, liberal Christian, Muslim, Buddhist, Hindu, New Ager, Jim Jones, and a host of devotees of other worldviews without changing very many words or concepts. I suspect that this would deeply trouble Paul and other writers of the Bible.

B. More specific comments in response to your statements

[Al noted several aspects of Myron's blog he appreciates, with some corrective points. He then continued on to say:] When you say, "From the Christian point of view, the truth about Christianity cannot be found in modern-styled objectivity," I get uneasy. That's because I feel that both you and Westphal (whom you cite here) have drunk too deeply at the Kierkegaardian well of existentialism, have too easily adopted the postmodern caricature of what previous writers (in any time period you might suggest) mean when they claim to have discovered some true facts, and have too quickly discarded the very possibility of knowledge of fact, at the urging of your postmodern mentors. I'm afraid the New Testament writers would not be impressed. Perhaps you could read again 1 Corinthians 15, especially verse 14. Our faith and our "kerygma, proclamation, or preaching" is in fact in vain if Christ is not in fact raised from the dead. Those who say otherwise should likely not properly be considered as proclaiming New Testament Christianity, even in the twenty-first century.

When you say, "A modern, objective approach to apologetic arguments also inclines Christian apologists to overlook the fact that their arguments may be used to support an oppressive and socially unjust form of Christianity, and therefore to that degree fail to justify *actual* Christianity," I ask: Could not the same be said of all Christian kerygma? Because kerygma, facts, and logic can be used for evil ends does not invalidate all use of kerygma, facts, and logic. Ever since Jesus spoke (particularly as recorded in John 13:35), love has been the hallmark of authentic Christianity. But as any responsible Christian parent understands, when people pursue false beliefs and immoral behaviors, the most loving response often is to urge them to correct such errors. Such corrections can take innumerable forms, including rational discussion, logic, and kerygma of many varieties in our "apologetic discourse." There is no need to create false dichotomies here—as postmodernists, existentialists, and others too often try to do (see Scott's helpful submission above). You seem to support that perspective in your passage: "The sort of kerygmatic apologetics I mean to endorse is one that takes lightly neither issues of truth nor the rationality of Christian belief. Biblically, the basis for and motivation of kerygma is love, and this means that at the core of a kerygmatic apologetic will be a love-centered rationality." Granted some kerygmatic (preached) apologetics does not very clearly manifest its love motivations. Passion for truth and right is too easily viewed in our culture as unloving. Thus, it seems to me that only a caricatured sense of "modern rationality" could prompt you to say, "What if we made love, and not modern rationality, the hallmark of our defense of Christianity, and took kerygma, not logic, as the form of our apologetic discourse?"—surely false dichotomies here. Of course humility is a basic Christian virtue (cf. 1 Corinthians 13:12). But note that expressions of confidence and conviction are too easily misconstrued as lacking in humility, including most expressions of "kerygmatic apologetics."

. . . I agree that "a kerygmatic apologetic will subsequently involve a particular person addressing a specific audience that has a concrete set of concerns about life, God, and the world." To me, this is not new (cf. David Clark, *Dialogical Apologetics* [Baker, 1993]), nor does it imply that "it will not deal in hypothetical questions or answers that do not arise from the context of the audience's lives and does not propose to offer answers that have not been personally won in the circumstances of the Christian's own life." It seems clear to me that a responsible address to any particular person's rejection of the Christian message at any point will normally require some advance preparation on such points, whether or not one has previously personally confronted difficulties with those points (e.g., God's creating the universe and all people). Such preparations (whether in formal education or in private reading and reflection) strike me as a practical demonstration of the love for doubters and unbelievers that you urge. For example, whether or not any given evangelical Christian has personally struggled with the conviction commonly taught in our public education systems that the universe (including the biosphere) is the product only of matter and the forces it generates, is it not an expression of responsible love to look into questions of whether the observed facts really demonstrate that this conviction is in fact true, in contrast to the Bible's affirmations on these matters?

I am quite uneasy with your statement, "An apostle does not present her message in the form of objective and universal truths, but as a confession of or witness to a personal word she has received from God." This world has seen too many of the type of Pastor Russell, Jim Jones, Joseph Smith, Mohammed, Buddha, etc. who were convinced that they had received "a personal word" from God. We really don't need any more such. Are you really willing to grant every JW, Mormon, liberal Christian, Muslim, Buddhist, Hindu, New Ager, Jim Jones, etc. equal unfettered freedom of "starting point for dialogue" without attempting to agree on any common ground for dialogue? If not, does not your "honestly confessing one's convictions and offering a starting point for dialogue" become a potentially unfruitful monologue? This world is likely already too full of witnesses eager to "determine the kind and shape" of their arguments, apologetic "dialogues," and "ways of being" in which they claim to "make sense." They can all appeal to the "eschatological character" of their perspectives, confident that in the end they will be shown to be right. Even if they and you acknowledge your "conclusions as finite, fallible, and penultimate," that remains rather unhelpful in this life where we all must make choices between unnumbered competing witnesses, each claiming eschatological justification "in which the truth is fully and finally revealed."

> Presuppositions of *method* versus those of *content* is a distinction often made by Christian apologists. *Presuppositions of method* are assumptions we make about how to find truth as we investigate the world; *presuppositions of content* are assumptions we have about the way the world actually is.

How can a "meganarrative (with global implications)" be qualitatively superior to any "metanarrative"? And how can anyone's metanarrative or meganarrative be actually presuppositionless? If some are naïve enough to think that their metanarrative or meganarrative is actually presuppositionless, I will not seek to defend them. Rather, I would prefer to note **presuppositions "of method" (not "of content")** which are unavoidable for anyone to discover/know any matter of fact, for example, 1) that knowledge is possible, 2) that the universe behaves regularly enough to make knowledge possible, and 3) that researchers need to behave honestly in their collections and interpretations of observations and arguments if they wish their conclusions to be taken seriously.

I agree that we need an apologetic that "addresses the whole person; that is, it is holistic . . . [including] social justice. . . . The goal, furthermore, is not one of rational domination but of 'winning' the person over." On the other hand, how will your announcing your own starting point without regard for your interlocutor's competing starting point help you win that person over? Also note that it is just too easy to accuse another who passionately presents an articulate perspective of seeking "rational domination." For example, Paul could likely be charged with this in Acts 26. Judging the motives of others is just too easy, and just too risky.

The rhetoric of "The loving one is already in agreement with [the enemy] . . . a battle of love or a battle in love! . . . the conciliatory spirit in love" didn't work for Kierkegaard, did it? Such rhetoric likely fails to take human depravity seriously enough. How can any evangelical Christian really honestly be in agreement with anyone with a contradictory worldview on issues other than whatever common ground we can establish in the process of loving open dialogue with them, such as presuppositions "of method" I mentioned above?

- Myron Bradley Penner: **Paul is *not* a modernist (but maybe sounds like a JW)!**

Al: Thanks for spending so much time drafting a response to my blog on postmodern apologetics. You clearly have thought much about these issues and your taking the time to draft such a careful response is appreciated. . . .

You begin by praising Scott for pointing out my false dichotomies, and to the extent that your comments are philosophically consonant with his you should refer to my response to him above. As a matter of fact, much of what I say to him goes for you too.

> *Neo-orthodoxy* was a twentieth-century theological movement that emerged from World War II, which emphasized God's transcendence and the inability of human reason to know God on its own.

I must first challenge you on your reading of Kierkegaard. While the early reception of Kierkegaard into English was conditioned primarily (philosophically) by the German and French existentialist reception of Kierkegaard (while theologically it was conditioned by Barth's and the **neo-orthodox** appropriation of Kierkegaard), that reading of Kierkegaard is largely viewed as inadequate at best and flat-out wrong at worst. Kierkegaard could hardly be described as a Sartrean existentialist, as you suggest, although parts of his writings certainly provided some impetus for existentialist philosophers. (See C. Stephen Evans' very good article on Kierkegaard in the *Cambridge Dictionary of Philosophy*, 2nd edition, ed. Robert Audi.) I must also say that it is a little difficult to accept your description of either Westphal's or my own appropriation of Kierkegaard as "uncritical." I would be a little more happy if you would just describe our use of Kierkegaard as "wrong" or "problematic."

Furthermore, you miscite Johannes Climacus (Kierkegaard's pseudonym). Climacus (in *Concluding Unscientific Postscript to Philosophical Fragments*)[1] asks us to imagine a pagan who prays sincerely to his false idol in his hut and an orthodox Christian "who lives in the midst of Christianity [and] enters, with knowledge of the true idea of God . . . the house of the true God and prays, but prays in untruth." Climacus then asks, "Where, then, is there more truth?"—on the side of the pagan who cries out for salvation to a false God, or with the insincere Christian who prays falsely to the true God? Climacus (or Kierkegaard) is not, in other words, claiming that the pagan is the exemplar of Christian faith—he in fact affirms in the next sentence that the pagan is "in truth worshipping an idol"—but Climacus is rather highlighting that getting it all right "objectively" is not the Christian concept of truth. In this case, the pagan embodies more of the Christian truth because at least the pagan realizes his need of salvation. I think we evangelicals typically express much the same thing in our talk of needing to have personal faith.

You find it deeply troubling that "most of [my] essay could be rewritten by a JW, Mormon, liberal Christian, Muslim, Buddhist, Hindu, New Ager, Jim Jones, and a host of other devotees of other worldviews without changing very many words or concepts." I am not quite as concerned about this as you. To begin with, this is an essay about apologetic method and not content, and insofar as these other groups you mention believe in God's revelation to human beings and the necessity of faith, I suppose there will be some overlap in methodology. Presumably you do not find it troubling that most of what evangelical apologists write—especially of the classical and evidential variety, but presuppositionalists too—could be written by a modern analytic philosopher. So what's the problem here? I am not saying that these other worldviews will end up being equally affirmed by the Christian apologist, although I am saying that there will not be as much "objective" (read: modern concept of objectivity) proof to sort them out. The point is that, measured by the modern notion of objectivity, Christian faith is objectively risky. I also believe that my intentional linking of kerygma to *agape* alleviates the legitimate concern you have with the wrongful use of revelation to endorse abusive, sick, and just plain false truth claims.

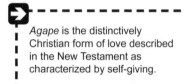

Agape is the distinctively Christian form of love described in the New Testament as characterized by self-giving.

You mention further on in your comments that the New Testament would not be impressed by my kerygmatic apologetics, but I am not sure I have given you an adequate understanding of my position. I appreciate the reminder to read 1 Corinthians 15, but I have read it a few times (even preached on it!) and I don't think a rereading will solve our dispute. As I mentioned in my response to Scott above, I see a clear distinction between claiming that p (p = any declarative sentence; for example, "The grass is green") is true—and even to have experienced p and on that basis to recommend belief in that p—and a claim to be able to demonstrate objectively that p in a manner that conforms to modern criteria for rationality. One cannot see Descartes, for example, being very impressed with Paul's claims in 1 Corinthians 15, or John's claims in the opening of 1 John.

I agree fully with your observation that the fact that "kerygma, facts, and logic can be used for evil ends does not invalidate all use of kerygma, facts, and logic." I have tried to say this same thing utilizing the Kierkegaardian phrase "the logic of insanity." And I trust your concern over my false dichotomies is sufficiently addressed above in my response to Scott.

One last point I will address from your comments concerns your questions regarding meganarratives and metanarratives. You asked, "How can a 'meganarrative (with global implications)' be qualitatively superior to any 'metanarrative'? And how can anyone's metanarrative or meganarrative be actually presuppositionless?" The second question first. As you point out, no one's story of the world can be presuppositionless, and that is the point of the critique of (or incredulity toward) metanarratives. The modern story of the world, based upon the paradigm of empirical science, seeks just such a presuppositionless story. So we substantially agree on this point. However, I do not quite agree with your endorsement of presuppositions of method versus those of content. A useful distinction, to be sure, but can we ever be completely neutral on content in our presuppositions about method? It doesn't seem so to me. Method presupposes some ideas about content. As long as we're all up-front about them (our presuppositions, that is), I am all for them!

As for your first question, the answer is that a meganarrative is about making as much sense of as much of our range of **phenomena** as possible, whereas a metanarrative is about claims to self-legitimacy—so that in the end it cuts off all avenues of rational discussion as to its validity. I think meganarratives are superior, then, because they acknowledge our situatedness but still make sense of life.

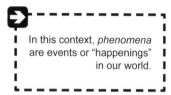

In this context, *phenomena* are events or "happenings" in our world.

As with Scott's comments, I find much of value in your response to me and trust that we can continue to move toward a greater mutual understanding. As you have been able to find substantial points of agreement with my point of view, so too I find myself in agreement with much that you endorse.

POSTMODERN MINISTRY:
IN SEARCH OF A LIVING ORTHODOXY

Ellen Haroutunian

In the opening of the film *The Fellowship of the Ring*,[1] Galadriel the elf queen sets the tone of the story as she tells us, "The world is changing. I see it in the water. I feel it in the earth. I smell it in the air." We are moved into the story with the sense that some things which once could be relied upon have changed and that something new will be required of the characters as they find their purpose along the journey.

Evangelicals also find ourselves in a world that has changed dramatically. Many ideas which we once believed to be "given" are now called into question. Increasingly we have found that we have lost our voice in a world of **pluralistic** expression. My friend Danny recalls a story from a Fuller Seminary professor who had been invited, along with other Christian leaders, to be at a screening for a new film, which explored themes of faith. After the film, the producers engaged in a long and passionate discussion about the 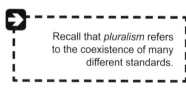 Recall that *pluralism* refers to the coexistence of many different standards. questions raised about faith and God with many of the invitees. Sadly, none of the Christians present were invited to that dialogue. The professor said afterward that "it was as though the producers felt they already knew what we were going to say." Often it seems that we have been so accustomed to expressing biblical truth in absolutist terms that we have lost the art of engaging in genuine conversation with people.

In this changing world, a new and honest look at ourselves may help us to rediscover what sort of people we need to be for the task that we face. Despite our care to keep our biblical truths uncompromised, we have sad evidence that Christians who have been well-versed in the Scriptures and ethics of family values are not living more uprightly than the "world."[2] Awash in the promises of modernism and its illusion of control and the lure of prosperity, we continually reinforce our own desires and dreams in the Word and worship. The gospel has become about maintaining our way of life. God is often remade in our image, instead of encountered as wholly, and Holy, Other.

We have forgotten about prophetic dreaming as our lives have curved inward. Thoughts of a truly holistic service for the sake of our community and the world have diminished. The story of Jesus—his life, death, and resurrection—have become "tokens of a purely personal hope."[3] Even our understanding of sin has shrunk to where we are more concerned with the bad influences of society than engagement with struggling hearts. Miroslav Volf says, "We want the kind of purity that wants the world cleansed of the 'other' rather than our hearts cleansed of the evil which drives others out."[4]

Postmodern people are seekers (though they allow the goal of their search to remain undefined). However, they seek not in our modern comfort zone of abstract truth, but in the flesh and blood reality of life. That is a path that would benefit us moderns as well. In C. S. Lewis' *The Horse and His Boy*, Bree the horse is musing about Aslan (the Christ figure) and the core beliefs of true Narnians. He tells the others not to be silly: Aslan is not a *real* lion, of course. Bree feels the tickle of a whisker by his ear and turns aghast to see find the giant lion standing beside him. "Horse, draw near," Aslan says. "Nearer still, my son. Do not dare not to dare. Smell me, touch me. Here are my paws, here is my tail, these are my whiskers. I am a true Beast."[5] Bree was quite a different horse after that. It is one thing to hold dear the truths of Christianity; it is quite another to encounter the living Word become flesh.

As unsettling as it is, a real dialogue with postmodernism can help us to recall more of our genuine Christian hope. John Milbank asks, "What if postmodernism is the misreading of the gospel beyond the law?"[6] We know that postmodernism eschews boundaries. It attempts to deconstruct hierarchies and level the playing field. Similarly, Jesus breaks down every dividing wall. He told us to call no man "Rabbi" or even "father" (Matthew 23:8–9). Paul adds that in Christ there is no culture, class, or gender (Galatians 3:28). Most shockingly, Christ broke down the wall between God's people and their "other," the uncircumcised (Ephesians 2:11–15). After being shown by God his own reluctance to allow that wall to crumble, the apostle Peter said, "God has shown me that I should not call any man impure or unclean" (Acts 10:28 NIV). This is stunning news for anyone who draws his or her identity from being in a position of power or entitlement. The gospel takes an ax to the roots of the false constructs of this world and reverses what we see as the natural order of things. The gospel makes room for the outcast and for those who have no power or voice.

We often think of a wrathful God whose fury is barely held back by the two wooden planks of the cross. But it seems that the wrath of God has the same purpose as his love. Both burn away that which keeps us from him and join together that which we have broken. Upon the death of Jesus, the veil which held back the Holy of Holies from the unclean world was ripped open and the holiness of God spilled out across the earth. Can we reimagine together what it will look like for us to live out a gospel like that, in which the Holy joyfully pours himself over the unholy? Are we willing to let him love and to love with him all of those whom he invites? To embrace both the red states and the blue states? The Moral Majorities and the Michael Moores? Can we sincerely offer a place at our table to the ones we have viewed, sometimes vehemently, as "other"? Our gospel says that our righteous God became sin—he became the pedophile, the murderer, the rapist, the gossip, the smug self-righteous one. He truly became the "other." We can begin to explore how "God's coming into this world of sin can inform the way in which we live in a world suffused with deception, injustice and violence."[7]

There is, of course, a marked difference between the postmodern extinguishing of boundaries, which can become a very dark "dissolving destructiveness,"[8] and the welcoming, liberating posture of the gospel. In Christ we have a powerful distinction and constraint. It is Christ in us, our hope of glory. Love resides in us and is the true necessary boundary, for love will never violate another, never usurp the role of God, and never allow us to violate ourselves. Love celebrates and nourishes the particularity of persons.

Our basic Christian orthodoxy, and what it says about Jesus, salvation, and the Scriptures, will always be true. But the tablets of our hearts are still being written upon. For us to survive as a church and, more importantly, to be successful in the transmission of our faith, we must be able to hand down a faith which not only informs but also encounters and transforms the heart. We must offer our living experience of the One who invites us to play at his feet, climb into his lap, and, perhaps, playfully tug at his beard. He is the One who wipes our tears with his two hands, opens our eyes with his spittle, chips away at our idols with his scars, nourishes us with his own body and blood.

The generations coming behind us are not ready to treasure our ideology, as we have, but postmodern people can still be moved by the heart. Our legacy is an incarnational faith, the God-man wrapped in our flesh. It is not a tame gospel. People will be stirred by an army of passion which moves across the land, not in an attitude of conquest for ourselves but as a people who embody his unstoppable love and who are breaking down every remaining wall of hatred, fear, division, and injustice in the name of Christ. As we reimagine along with God, who so loves the world, we can recover big dreams. Maybe it is as simple as making friends across some of the many divides. Or it could be as outrageous as the suggestion of my friend Peter, a wildly imaginative pastor, who asks, "What if a thousand of us American, middle-class white guys went to the Sudan and died alongside those who are being exterminated by slow genocide? Would the world pay attention then?"

We can reimagine what it means to move into the world, not with a cross to crucify but as those who are crucified with Christ. Christian orthodoxy will always stand. It is time for us to reimagine orthodoxy, not as a what but as a Who. Jesus says, "I am the Truth." He cannot be contained or defined. The lovely urn which contained our untouchable heirloom faith is busted wide open. He is not here; he is risen.

MINISTRY IN THE NOW

Ellen Haroutunian

I can appreciate the irony in attempting to write about ministry to postmodern people in the midst of a culture in which "how to's" are viewed to be as reliable as the wind. Of course there is no one prototype or model for the emerging church. The look of the church which ministers to postmoderns is as varied as the people it serves. However, I believe we can explore a posture of the heart through which the imagining of possibilities can flow.

The ministers who have found a voice in postmodern ministry are shepherds of the soul. They are effective not by establishing goals and maintaining a position of power, but by valuing and pursuing relationships and trust along a journey walked in community. The "end" of the journey is Jesus but the means is a compassionate sensibility. The first thing we must do is to learn to listen.

One way to listen is to pay attention to postmodern art. The creative and thoroughly postmodern film, *Eternal Sunshine of the Spotless Mind*,[9] offers one key to the hearts of people in this age. The film portrays quirky characters who are stuck in time with only their own passions to give them meaning. They cannot bear the pain of loving a real, flawed person, yet cannot bear to be alone. They find meager hope in a new memory-erasing technology designed to eliminate the pain of life. The story explores the cruel despair born from this futile way of living.

The two main characters have attempted to erase each other from their minds after a failed and often dysfunctional love affair. However, even as audiotapes play in the background in which each character describes a whole catalog of offenses committed by the other, they decide to reunite and risk love again. Many in our film discussion group felt discouraged at an ending that left us feeling so ambivalent because the characters were sure to face the same, insurmountable problems again. Yet one young woman said to me, "I want to be known and loved just as I am, too. Isn't this what we all want?" She reflected the longings of the postmodern heart as she began to wonder about Jesus. He's the one who knows our cache of failures and woes and says, "I want to be with you."

Over and over again, people who are adrift in the postmodern culture reveal themselves to be longing for that kind of love. It's easy for modern Christians to fret over the postmodern thinker's lack of belief in an overarching truth which can guide some sense of moral rightness. Yet, it may be more important to remember that people are often betrayed by their own hearts. None of us can erase or avoid what is most true about us. The desire to be loved, the hope for what's wrong in our lives to be made right, and the thirst for a larger sense of connection which offers some sense of wholeness all find their way to the surface of the heart, in one form or another. The longing for God is very present in lonely human beings.

In *Eternal Sunshine*, the story is told both forward and backward simultaneously, expressing the dilemma of postmodern people. There are no universal patterns to trust, not even the concept of time. Internal disconnect and despair are portrayed in the lead female character who "puts on her personality with her hair color." In an attempt to reach out to someone like her, we must recognize that postmoderns have already said "no thanks" to Christianity because our assumption of absolute truth carries no weight with them. For many, the word *Christian* has come to mean close-minded and judgmental, and trust has been lost. Trust must be rebuilt through friendship and the willingness to walk a long journey alongside them filled with genuine curiosity and conversation.

In the film *Garden State*,[10] a young man named Andrew Largeman is wanting to wake up and find what is real and authentic after living much of his young life numbed by medications given to him by his psychiatrist father. He had been treated as a problem, not a person. He finds some hope in becoming attuned to himself enough so that he can begin to love a young woman and invite her along in his journey of awakening. At one point in the film, "Large" and his friends come upon a giant hole that has opened up where a new shopping mall was to have been built in town. It is frightening and seems bottomless. A security guard lives on the chasm's edge and the friends nickname him "the guardian of the infinite abyss." They marvel that he can bear living so close to it. The "guardian" replies that with the love of his wife and baby, he can feel at home anywhere. After this exchange, Large and friends go to the edge and scream into the chasm. Postmoderns concede that there is mystery that is far beyond explanation and control. They don't know whether to embrace or fear it; but if they find any hope in facing this giant unknown, it is the companionship that they find along the way. Love seems to be the most "real" thing they can find. For people who have such an incohesive sense of themselves and the world, the great opportunity for ministry is to create places for people to belong.

We have seen over and over in ministry that belonging precedes believing. The culture is rife with dysfunctional relationships and highly disconnected people. It is market-driven and everything, including people, is viewed with exchange value in mind. Can it compete, will it sell, will it win? To be pointing people toward Jesus is to be inviting them into our communal life and loving them just because they *are*. Building trust and safe relationships helps to create a sense of home, connection, and a belief in a person's inherent value to God.

Through the inherent despair in postmodern reality, a spiritual hunger is deepening. Unlike the time when "seeker sensitive" strategies were designed to reach skittish, cynical moderns, we can be unabashedly spiritual and open in our worship as we invite others in. We can enjoy a wide variety of music and "relevant to the culture" expressions in worship, because God reveals himself in many ways. While not eliminating teaching, the sermons at our church are primarily descriptions of Jesus and what he's like in Bible stories and in our own stories. However, the focal point in every service is the Communion table. Everything—the singing, the sermon, the art—is leading up to this point. Through this simple meal we are telling his story again. There is an air of weightiness that says that this simple meal is about something far greater than ourselves. It's a quiet, unpressured invitation which says, simply, "If you want Jesus, come." In the context of this place of belonging and home, the spiritually seeking postmodern person can begin to dare to stretch out in what seems to be a frightening, infinite abyss and find the face, arms, and heart of God. The writer and apostle Paul said that in God we all live and move and have our being, and we can reach out and grope and find him, for he is not far from each one of us (Acts 17:27–28). When the time is right, postmodern people who have been grasping at anything and everything receive Jesus' substance into their emptiness.

We need to be trusting that Jesus is indeed at work, pursuing relationship with people, and that we don't need to force the process or make it conform to a modern idea of how faith is realized. A young man who considered himself to be an atheist came to church and listened to sermons, participated in movie discussions and other parts of church life, and resisted constant goading by his atheist friends who claimed he'd be committing intellectual suicide to believe in such nonsense. We saw his heart respond to Christ long before his intellect could give assent. Overcome by the presence of Jesus he experienced through the love of his people, he chose to join us in Communion one day. He called us a few days later. Having never taken Communion before, he had torn off a piece of bread that was far too big. He ate some and put the rest in his pocket. "What do I do?" he pleaded. He didn't want to throw out the body of Christ. His anguish still warms my heart. He really *believed.* "Jesus will remain with you," we said. "And yes, it's OK to toss that out."

> *Pragmatism* focuses on usefulness or what works, rather than what is good or true.
>
> *Hierarchical attitudes* here refers to attitudes that rate people on a scale where some people are higher and others are lower.

God is leading us from a results-oriented **pragmatism** in ministry toward a relational offering of Christ's heart and engagement with his family. Ministry is truly more a matter of authenticity of heart than a style or program. In our church we've learned not to take ourselves too seriously as we try to figure out what it means to offer ourselves in love. Ministry flows from the wonder that Jesus has somehow created a "we," a communal, sacred space into which we can invite others. Ministers do not need to be managers of all this, but can be shepherds and facilitators for the people as they seek to create this community. We need both men and women in vital, up-front positions, belying the older, **hierarchical attitudes** of the modern era. Most importantly, people who lead and minister need to be people of substance who are deeply connected on the journey themselves and who have immersed themselves in intimacy with Jesus.

On a billboard near my home a local church advertises that they are "committed to your success." They believe the modern "American dream" which says that hope is prosperity. They are trying to offer quick fixes and answers to a nation that has experienced terrorist attacks and horrific natural disasters such as the recent hurricane, Katrina. With the absence of ideologies to explain things, postmoderns seem to be more ready than modern Christians to acknowledge the harsh realities of injustice, the apparent randomness of the universe, and evil. Detweiler and Taylor say that "for postmoderns, the road to heaven must go through hell."[11] Jesus was known as the Man of Sorrows, and his suffering and loneliness can speak to lonely, disenfranchised people. We can walk with him there. Ministry is about revealing Jesus. He is the light in the postmodern darkness.

COMMENTS

• Scott Morizot: **Life within the storm**

"There is, of course, a marked difference between the postmodern extinguishing of boundaries, which can become a very dark 'dissolving destructiveness,' and the welcoming, liberating posture of the gospel. In Christ we have a powerful distinction and constraint. It is Christ in us, our hope of glory."

[Ellen's words here] struck me as such a key statement. In other threads, people have commented on the fact that the philosophy called "postmodern" is an attempt to capture essential changes in the way that people experience and interact with the world around them. I am one of those who do not experience the world in the same way as those whom we tend to label as more modern, nor did I grow up immersed in the evangelical culture. And I recently tried to explain to some friends some of those core differences by pointing out that I do not experience change in the same way. I've noticed over the years that people like me do not seem to experience pain or stress simply from change as other people do. (Of course, a change that is inherently painful is still pain, but not because it is change.) And at the heart of that seems to be the fact that there is always a part of me that is continuously deconstructing, qualifying, discounting, and evaluating everything new I encounter, as well as those things I currently believe. And there is relatively little pain in shifting things around.

This seems very different from those who experience pain simply from the process of experiencing change or a shift in circumstances or belief. Theirs is a system that resists change. Ours is a system that is very fluid, but instead strongly resists becoming less fluid. In our world today, that has a lot of strengths, but (as someone who has been there) it can definitely become *a very dark dissolving destructiveness*. That phrase truly captures it. And in the midst of that maelstrom, Christ can set himself as an anchor, can build belief that will not change, can provide the central rock to which we can cling.

To try to illustrate, I pointed out that my friends seem to be able to fairly easily hold 538 (I just picked what seemed to me to be a huge number) firm convictions or beliefs. And they can experience some degree of stress adapting or changing any of them. By contrast, it can be very hard for me to deeply anchor five rocks or convictions along with Jesus. The character of the struggle is very different. But the hope at the center is Jesus. It can't be all intellectual or ideological. That just doesn't do a whole lot for me. But the heart of Jesus and Christianity? Wow! Thanks for capturing it.

- Ellen Haroutunian: **Illusions of certainty and fluid systems of thought**

Scott: I appreciate your sharing of your personal experience as you negotiate life and faith! Your statement, "This seems very different from those who experience pain simply from the process of experiencing change or a shift in circumstances or belief. Theirs is a system that resists change. Ours is a system that is very fluid, but instead strongly resists becoming less fluid" hit an interesting point that may be common to both systems of thought. As one who had been educated in a modernistic approach to theology, I sensed that the resistance to change in that system often came from a fear of loss of control. The propositional truths that explain God, people, and life helped to create an illusion of certainty which seemed to reduce mystery and suffering in our lives. Similarly, I wonder if the resistance toward becoming less fluid that is felt by postmodern thinkers can be the other side of the same coin. There is still a sense of control in the desire to be the one who gets to decide what is true. I am curious about your thoughts on that.

However, I do find a more fluid system of thought and "being" much more inviting and conducive to being a follower of Jesus. As a woman, I had found the more static system of thought to be damaging at times because it limited my understanding of myself as the feminine image of God (Genesis 1:26), and even reduced my experience of God's lavish heart. One of the more hopeful aspects of postmodern thought is that it is helping us former modernists to tease apart our propositional truths from the reality of Jesus himself. The older I get, the more

I realize that there's probably only a handful of truths that I'd die for, and all of them spring from Jesus.

Thanks, Bro. Ellen

- Scott Morizot: **Who decides what is true?**

[Ellen: You wrote:] "Similarly, I wonder if the resistance toward becoming less fluid that is felt by postmodern thinkers can be the other side of the same coin. There is still a sense of control in the desire to be the one who gets to decide what is true. I am curious about your thoughts on that."

It is certainly a way to cope with change and uncertainty, and I suppose there is an element of control. And there is certainly often a choice of what to believe (which seems to carry a similar meaning to "true" in this context). On the other hand, since ideas and beliefs can (and do) often shift in response to external factors rather than choice, the more fluid system doesn't appear to offer as much control. At the same time, I've recently noticed that I now appear to be struggling with some beliefs I think are true but would rather not believe. While I do recall the "dark dissolving destructiveness" (love that phrase) of a fluid system without the center or rock that Jesus provides, I don't recall ever having to struggle with beliefs I found I had but didn't want. So your point probably has considerable merit.

I still find my intellectual attachment to "truths" I think I know is less firm than those truths I have experienced, starting with the truth that God is. Dreams speak more to me than statements, even statements of truth. The tangible love I receive or give means more to me than being right. All of those, in small steps through different people and then directly, are how Jesus drew me to/back to him as he anchored my life and spirit. Yes, he certainly breaks down walls. And I do see lots of walls all through and around the church. At the same time, he promises to be the stable foundation and the anchoring cornerstone to those of us who need at least a few walls.

Although that one paragraph stopped me and spurred my initial response, I can't express how much your whole essay spoke to me. Thank you. Scott

- Rick Abele: **A postmodern call to action**

Ellen: I have to compliment you on one of the clearest and most excellent little essays on where I personally would like to see this thing go. Will we, as the next generation, continue to sit in front of our computers blogging and bantering, or will we actually "go" to Sudan or to Pakistan or Chechnya or wherever to give our lives for others? So far, in this "movement" there's been a lot of talk, a lot of name-making, and already a lot of hero worship, yet minimal action. Indeed we are in the early stages of one the most revolutionary, world-changing periods in the last several hundred years. As militant Islam continues to froth, churn, and spread across the nations, when will God's army of faceless foot soldiers rise up as a response to Satan's army? What will it take for this generation to rise up and respond to those who gladly give their lives for the sake of sending another infidel to hell, and who will instead die to help even one find The Way to eternal glory? Thanks for your post.

- Brian McLaren: **Jolting poetry**

Ellen's posting, I think all who read it will agree, was beautiful to the point of poetry. And that beauty itself says something important about ministry in a postmodern context. We must humbly seek and portray truth (as we've been discussing in other threads). And we must also seek and portray beauty. I think of Jesus' words about the woman who anointed his feet with tears and perfume: "She has done a beautiful thing." But truth and beauty (as Aristotle realized) are two-thirds of a trinity that also requires goodness. That combination, in Ellen's words, is a truly big dream.

She said, "As we reimagine along with God, who so loves the world, we can recover big dreams. Maybe it is as simple as making friends across some of the many divides. Or it could be as outrageous as the suggestion of my friend Peter, a wildly imaginative pastor, who asks, 'What if a thousand of us American, middle-class white guys went to the Sudan and died alongside those who are being exterminated by slow genocide? Would the world pay attention then?'"

That last sentence won't let me go. Is there a mission agency that would take up this kind of mission? Is there an individual willing to lead it? My guess is that if just one of us had the courage to lead a mission like this, a thousand people would be willing to follow. Now practically, adding a thousand mouths to feed in Darfur might not be that helpful. So maybe a hundred would be more realistic. But where could the other nine hundred go? Among the Palestinians whose plight is too often ignored by Christians of a certain misguided eschatology? Maybe into Colombia, where drug lords terrorize people in the jungles? Or maybe just into downtown Camden, New Jersey, where life is hard and people are too easily forgotten.

I'm writing this in the days after Hurricane Katrina. I am mindful of the unease in my country that because so many of the people of the Gulf Coast were poor and black, it was easier to be sluggish in responding to their emergency than if they had been rich and white. I am thinking of the incarnation, how "God-with-us" means that when the hurricane hits, God hasn't evacuated, but suffers with us, and will be sure we are not forgotten. There are groups doing this sort of outrageous thing. The Christian Peacemaker teams, for example. Or Camden House and Simple Way and Ruthba House and Communality. May they inspire us all, not just to admire them, but to imitate their faith.

Thank you, Ellen, for this moving poetry—and the jolting challenge it carries.

- Myron Bradley Penner: **Ironizing postmodern irony**

Ellen has articulately (and even, as Brian notes, poetically) recommended postmodernism as a cure for a particular type of malaise that often infects modern forms of Christian ministry. But, like **Plato's** *pharmakon* or chemotherapy, what cures you when you are ill will kill you when you are well. A good dose of postmodernism will inoculate us against the modern trap of viewing ministry in formulaic and impersonal terms. The modern worldview,

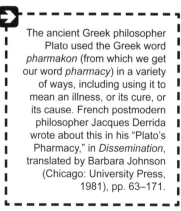

The ancient Greek philosopher Plato used the Greek word *pharmakon* (from which we get our word *pharmacy*) in a variety of ways, including using it to mean an illness, or its cure, or its cause. French postmodern philosopher Jacques Derrida wrote about this in his "Plato's Pharmacy," in *Dissemination*, translated by Barbara Johnson (Chicago: University Press, 1981), pp. 63–171.

with its emphasis on **empirical science** (to be distinguished from its predecessor, **natural science**) as the only authoritative source of truth and what is most important in the universe, naturally led to an emphasis on technology, as the application of scientific discovery to control and master the physical universe. One of the deepest ironies of the modern era has been that the hyperconsciousness of individual subjectivity has produced a greater sense of personal isolation and loss of identity. Unfortunately, Christians have also increasingly looked to technology and the vagaries of the empirical science paradigm to provide us with "tools" that maximize our ministry efficiencies in ways that mimic the ironies of modern life. The result often has been that the same sort of rootlessness and impersonal ("objective") forms of engagement characterize our ministry efforts in modernity as generally characterize the practices and institutions of our wider modern Western culture. Into this situation, a little postmodern irony is helpful—but, as Kierkegaard reminds us (and Ellen does too), irony can also be a sickness if it is not situated within the overall context of a life subjectively engaged in pursuing the truth. We must ironize our irony too.

> **➜** *Empirical science* is the modern view of science as based (only) on what we know through the five senses.
>
> Before modernity, *natural science* accepted that there are certain assumptions that are necessary to the task of knowing and discovering the world.

I deeply appreciate and resonate with Ellen's call for us to see bodies, and not just souls; persons, and not just problems; faces, and not just unbelievers; as we minister the gospel of Jesus Christ in a postmodern context.

• Ellen Haroutunian: **The grace of postmodernism**

Myron: I like the phrase "we must ironize our irony." You are so right. This came to mind as I was watching a movie about the life of Luther last weekend. The movement from the traditional, premodern worldview to the age of reason was often a violent one, exposing the fear and the darkness of hearts within the church which prized control and power over surrender and trust.

And here we go again! The entrance of a changing worldview has once again exposed idolatry and the fear of loss of control and certainty. How can we be informed by what went before as we face the challenge of ministering in this new world? As you say, it would be in our subjective pursuit of truth, which would include a willingness to see Jesus as he reveals himself in these times.

I am uncomfortable, though, with thinking of postmodernism as a "cure" on any level. I think that idea gives more substance to the concept than it merits. What I do see within it, however, is a particular grace afforded to us because of the healthy questioning which postmodernism demands. I am saddened, though not surprised, to see that many evangelicals do not seem to think we can handle some self-examination.

The grace I see in this situation is that engaging with postmodern thought exposes some of the idolatries which evangelicals have embraced in our well-meaning attempt to combat a too-liberal interpretation of the faith and Scriptures. Reliance on propositions and doctrine subtly appeals to the same ignoble attraction that was presented to humankind by the serpent in the garden at the very beginning of our story. Has our modernized evangelical approach not quietly dethroned God as the source of life and truth, and thereby reduced community to a group that must agree intellectually but yet remain solitary and unknown to one another?

- Myron Bradley Penner: **A postmodern cure?**

Ellen: I certainly agree with you that postmodernism can be a grace of God in our lives. Perhaps I should explain better what I meant in my last post. A certain amount of postmodernism is necessary for some—especially those of us in the modern, (post)evangelical, and increasingly post-Christian West—and I think it will cure certain forms of intellectual diseases. I think that postmodern criticisms of modernity are an important corrective, but I am unwilling to call it an un-qualified good. Saying postmodernism is inherently good seems to lack a certain necessary consciousness of our own situatedness.

BTW: I find the underlying ambiguity toward postmodernism in Kenzo's blog, "Evangelical Faith and (Postmodern) Others"—Is he for it or against it?—quite interesting and very telling in this regard. I think the (postmodern) truths we seize upon in our context will look quite different, and be expressed quite differently, in another context. Of course, in very practical terms, postmodern irony will not take us very far into God's grace if either we have not been jaded by the modernization

Iconoclasm literally refers to the destruction of religious icons and symbols; here it is used more generally to refer to the postmodern tendency to tear down modern ideas and be skeptical about knowledge and truth.

process or we are hopelessly trapped in its cynicism. Unrestrained **iconoclasm** will eventually end up like the proverbial wolf that ate himself. (So I think we agree on that too.)

• Paula Spurr: **A new kind of action**

The comments on Ellen's blog remind me of a conversation I had with a college professor of mine, way back in 1985. I was commenting to him how interesting it was that the church thrives in places where it is sometimes hardest oppressed, and wondering out loud whether what we needed in Canada (indeed, all of North America) was a little good old-fashioned oppression to wake up the lukewarm church. He immediately responded with a "Heavens, no!! Be thankful for the blessings we have!!" I disagreed with him then, but chose to end the conversation. Why did my comments make him so uncomfortable? Did the thought of suffering for the gospel threaten his standard of living?

OK, low blow. But that whole conversation seems to me a good picture of the difference between the modern and postmodern approach to doing church. I wanted to get in there, get dirty, truly experience what I believe. He wanted to be thankful to God for three square meals a day plus dessert and a nice car, and especially be thankful to God that he didn't have to be persecuted for what he believed. Which leads me to the question: Wasn't my professor wrong? Didn't Jesus call us to take up our cross and follow him? His language was always "sell it all," "leave your mother and father," very provocative language. Surely he meant it.

I agree with Brian: it *is* time for action. Having grown up in the evangelical church, I have heard that before; and action usually meant, "Time to learn the Romans Road, practice up my witnessing skills, and start knocking on some doors to tell them about Jesus." I dream of a new kind of action. I want to cultivate the friendship our family has begun with a Buddhist family that moved here from Nepal. I want to meet my neighbors, I want to invite a single mom over to my house to help me make wine, I want to turn my ugly back alley into a flower garden because Beauty matters. I want to be Good. I don't care too much anymore about being Right. (I know I'm paraphrasing somebody there, probably Mr. McLaren; I'm so sorry I didn't take better notes when my mind was being blown by all the great books I've read lately!)

• Viki: **Getting off the treadmill**

Amen, Paula. Someone once said that the final test of faith isn't what we believe, but how much we love. Having struggled for years to be Right, it is a relief to climb off that treadmill. Having said that, being Good is much, much harder in some ways. It's about being Christlike and Christ-centered. It's about outworking the principle of "Love God and love your neighbor with all that's in you," and translating that into everything you say and do and think, until love flows from you with every exhalation. Let no one say this is easy.

• Paula Spurr: **Loving = living faith out**

This certainly is *not* easy!! Thank you for adding that. Having an opinion about love is much easier than really loving someone. Anybody else thinking about the first few verses in 1 Corinthians 13 here?

If I invite that single mom over, she *is* going to ask me to babysit, and if she doesn't ask I will offer—and what if her kids are very difficult to watch?

If I cultivate that friendship with my Buddhist neighbour, my daughter and his son are going to play, and my daughter is going to come to me with some wonderful, yet difficult, questions about faith and life.

If I plant that garden in the gravel of my back alley, there are going to be some serious weeds and thistles to pull.

I am going to have to quit being so lazy!! I am going to have to think of others more highly than myself. I am going to need to go to God moment by moment to have the strength and wisdom to keep these commitments and answer these questions. That sounds like faith being lived out to me! Don't get me wrong; I'm not there yet. I'm very selfish and lazy, but God is working on me, bit by bit.

- Ellen Haroutunian: **Christ, the "great iconoclast"**

He is indeed at work! It would be fun to dialogue about what it means to continue to grow "eyes to see" Christ at work in this world. C. S. Lewis has called him the "great iconoclast." I imagine he will really stretch our categories of understanding, if we allow it.

[BTW] Paula, I love your passion! It is in the type of things you describe that we will discover anew and give weight to truth as he reveals himself over and over again, in our midst.

SPIRITUAL FORMATION IN A POSTMODERN CONTEXT

Brian McLaren

"Spiritual formation" is a new term for many—it's already a buzzword in some circles. It has a long and noble history among Roman Catholics, but has in recent years grown in popularity among both conservative and traditional (or mainline) Protestants. In many ways, it provides an alternative to or advancement beyond the terms *Christian education*, *Discipleship*, and *Follow-up*. These three terms have a special rootedness in the late modernity of the postwar period.

- *Christian education* meant an approach to Christian training that generally mirrored modern public school education. It was age-graded, teacher-focused, classroom-situated, and curriculum-based. It was equally valued in both traditional and conservative Protestant churches, and was often equivalent to "Sunday school for adults."

- *Discipleship* was modeled more on self-study correspondence courses than public school classrooms. It generally involved fill-in-the-blanks booklets which one would complete on one's own by reading Bible verses (generally disconnected from any narrative context) and answering questions. The result was that one would gradually absorb a systematic theology. But discipleship usually added an important new dimension: mentoring. The discipler met regularly (usually weekly) with the disciple, taking a personal interest in the disciple—not only seeing that he had completed his lessons and gotten the right answers, but also being available to answer questions, offer encouragement, and introduce and monitor progress in other spiritual practices (such as the "daily quiet time"). And the best of the discipleship **curricula** went beyond fill-in-the-blank answers: for example, engaging students in writing their own paraphrases of extended Bible passages or asking them to reflect on their lives.

- *Follow-up* generally meant helping people who had "prayed to receive Christ" or "made a decision for Christ"—often at a mass evangelism crusade—to confirm their decision. It was nearly unheard of in traditional Protestant settings, but was commonplace among conservative Protestants with a **revivalistic** emphasis. Having responded to a revivalistic "invitation," one would be counseled to obtain "assurance of salvation" and be instructed in four requirements for ongoing spiritual growth: to pray, read the Bible, witness, and attend a Bible-believing congregation. Follow-up was in many ways a minimalist, short-term (often one-session) introduction to and overview of discipleship.

> *Curricula* means "different programs of study."
>
> *Revivalistic* is a reference to "revival meetings," where an emphasis is placed on making public, life-changing spiritual decisions and commitments, particularly decisions to be "born again."

These modern methods probably arose to solve the apparent failure of a previous methodology that we might describe as the institutional participation model of spiritual growth: *institutional participation = spiritual health.* In other words, attend the required Sunday and holiday services, participate in the expected rituals or program, and you will be spiritually fine. Perhaps this approach was considered sufficient when small towns, schools, and families all supported a certain understanding of Christian living. But with the urbanization of American, the profusion of entertainment media, and the strengthening of secularization in the late twentieth century, increasing numbers of Christians found that *institutional participation + 0 = **nominalism** – spiritual vitality,* or *institutional participation + 0 = spiritual ill health.*

So Christian education, discipleship, and follow-up methodologies were developed, and no doubt they have helped countless people. My own spiritual life has been deeply impacted by all three. All three methods seemed to share common educational assumptions: right knowledge would lead to right behavior, and more knowledge would lead to better behavior—or *knowledge = growth.* For this reason, these three methods could together be called the knowledge acquisition approach. Meanwhile, in many holiness, charismatic, and Pentecostal circles intense emotional experiences were valued in place of knowledge. The more experiences one acquires, the better off one will be: *spiritual experiences = growth.* In recent years, many individuals and churches have hybridized these two approaches, creating what is probably becoming the dominant formula in conservative Protestant settings: *knowledge + spiritual experiences = growth.*

However, some degree of disillusionment has set in with the knowledge and experience acquisition approaches, just as it did with institutional participation. A number of factors have contributed to this disillusionment, including boredom, pride over mastery of information (or experiences) without a corresponding transformation in character, a tendency to drift into **esoteric** or theoretical concerns far removed from real life, a focus on in-

> *Nominalism* literally means "existing in name only."
>
> *Esoteric* refers to knowledge that is highly abstract or difficult to comprehend.
>
> *Monastic* refers to monasteries, which, from the third century AD on, have been closed communities of people who have taken certain vows and are dedicated to work and prayer.

formation that kept people from making satisfying interpersonal contact, superficiality, a sense that curricula and teaching methods were outdated, and a kind of consumer mentality where people were always shopping for the latest, greatest seminar, teaching series, or revival.

In their place, a more holistic concept of spiritual formation has begun to emerge—drawing both from **monastic** and other Roman Catholic sources and drawing from contemporary philosophy and educational theory as well. This approach questions the assumptions of institutional participation and knowledge or experience acquisition. Instead, it proceeds from a more nuanced understanding that *knowledge + experiences + relationships + practices + suffering + service + time = growth + health.* This approach has several characteristics:

1. Knowledge or information is not considered unimportant. But in an era of training videos and DVDs, CDs and tapes, websites and podcasts, not to mention radio and TV, information has become **ubiquitous**, and information transmission at the speed of speech is considered inefficient and in fact a waste of time, especially when one must drive to a fixed location to receive it—without the possibility of multitasking (i.e.,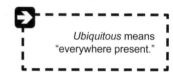

   Ubiquitous means "everywhere present."

   acquiring information while driving, exercising, doing household chores, etc.). Information in this context must be conveyed in an anywhere-anytime manner, and with higher efficiency than traditional lectures, sermons, or classes. And the learner must be encouraged to actively think for herself, evaluate based on her own experience and previous learning, and apply information to her own life rather than simply taking in information passively as if from an IV tube to the memory.

2. Experiences are also not considered unimportant. However, in an age of media, hype, marketing, and political spin, manipulation is ubiquitous, and so experiences must not even appear to be forced in order to be considered legitimate. If overstatement and pressure were typical in many Pentecostal/charismatic settings, now understatement and "space" become the essential contexts for genuine experiences. For these reasons, we're seeing a growing interest in contemplative practices, where God is found in the center of normalcy, not only beyond its edges as tended to be the case in charismatic contexts.

3. Relationships were gaining importance in the modern discipleship model, but now they become even more important. Instead of existing to be the transmitter of information, the relationship

between mentor and apprentice itself becomes part of the curriculum. It is no wonder that the roles of *anam cara* ("soul-friend" in Gaelic) and spiritual director (drawing from the **Benedictine** tradition) are experiencing an unprecedented upsurge. These roles involve not primarily speaking/presenting, but rather listening and being

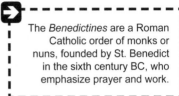

The *Benedictines* are a Roman Catholic order of monks or nuns, founded by St. Benedict in the sixth century BC, who emphasize prayer and work.

present. The spiritual director's personal knowledge of the person being helped and his or her personal knowledge of God become as important as the "objective" information available to be transmitted.

4.   The modern follow-up and discipleship models both had some degree of emphasis on practices (pray and read your Bible in a daily quiet time, witness, attend church). But the value of these practices lay largely in their means to the end of gaining more knowledge. The monastic tradition offers a new repertoire of practices whose function is not in acquiring knowledge but rather in acquiring mastery of the self. For example, fasting masters appetites and impulses. Contemplation and meditation master attention. Silence and solitude master pride. Simplicity, generosity, and hospitality master greed. But these practices do more than master the self: they also develop faculties much as exercise develops muscles—concentration, discernment, awareness of the presence of God, humility, and so on. Rather than making character transformation and spiritual aptitude an assumed byproduct of knowledge, practices make character transformation and spiritual aptitude a primary goal.

5.   Suffering was certainly acknowledged as a reality in the knowledge acquisition approach, although, with proper knowledge, perhaps some or all of it could be avoided or minimized. But in spiritual formation, experiences of suffering are seen as essential

to the development of virtue. For example, without suffering fear, there is no courage. Without suffering annoyance, there is no longsuffering or forbearance. Without suffering injury, there is no mercy or forgiveness. Add to this a resurgence of attention to the "dark night of the soul," and it is clear that suffering is not seen as an interruption to spiritual growth but rather a requirement for certain dimensions of it.

6.   Service—not only *within* or *for* the church, but also *as* the church working for the good of the world—is increasingly seen as being indispensable to authentic spiritual growth and health.

7.   Adding the element of time to the equation undercuts a modern concern for speed and efficiency. The goal isn't to become mature as fast as possible, since such an approach to growth is seen as immature and therefore antithetical to true growth. Rather, the goal is to experience the seasons of life in such a way that one is formed, through time, in the context of normal life experiences. One seeks less to fill in the blanks of a book but rather to fill in one's days with meaningful interaction with God, others, and self. Time is seen as a good part of God's good creation to be enjoyed and savored, not as a clock to be beaten.

Each approach to spiritual growth and health has its own theological roots or context. As far as I can tell, at this point the practice of spiritual formation is often being undertaken without much theological reflection. As a result, spiritual formation practices are often grafted onto old and potentially incompatible theologies. It remains to be seen whether spiritual formation can function as an add-on to just any theology. However, a "practice before theory" approach may in fact be fitting; it may be that a better theology of spiritual formation can only be developed **iteratively** with the practice itself.

> *Iteratively* refers to the repetition of something.
>
> *Panacea* = cure for anything and everything.

I do not wish to present spiritual formation as a **panacea**. It remains to be seen how well this approach will work in producing truly transformed people, especially people who come to faith from unchurched backgrounds. It also remains to be seen how well this approach will work for people in diverse cultural settings—from affluent Hong Kong to rural Zimbabwe, from urban Buenos Aires to postmodern Scandanavia. Finally, it remains to be seen how effective a spiritual formation approach will be in the long-term development of children and adolescents as lifelong Christian disciples. Even so, in light of the problems with institutional participation and knowledge or experience acquisition approaches, I see the move toward spiritual formation as hopeful and promising. My personal experience—both in my own life and in the church where I serve—confirms my hope.

COMMENTS

• Scot McKnight: **Holy Spirit and relationships at the center**

Brian: Thanks for this comprehensive approach to the elements that come into focus as spiritual formation takes place. A crucial component from a New Testament perspective would be the centrality of the Holy Spirit in the process, and one might want to argue that these are elements the Holy Spirit appropriates as humans are remade into the image of God through the gospel.

Another element for me is that there has come in our day a new understanding of education, which is in part much of what is going on in all spiritual formation perceptions by Christians, and this new understanding of education is more along a holistic **telos**. In other words, we are no longer permitted (as professors) to "inform" students simply by "lecturing" to them and then "testing" them to see if they have "learned" what they should know. More and more, the outcome-based educational theory asks us to describe what we want our students to be able to "do" when they finish our course or our major or our school, and then everything has to be shaped to develop those outcomes if we wish to be genuinely an educational institution.

> Recall that *telos* means "end, goal, or purpose."
>
> The *Shema-Jesus Creed tradition* refers to the ancient Jewish practice of saying the *shema*, which literally means "hear," from Deuteronomy 6:4–5, "Hear, O Israel, the LORD your God is one. Love the LORD your God"—twice daily. Jesus affirmed the *shema* in the New Testament, in Mark 12:29–31, adding to it the command to love one's neighbor as oneself. See Scot McKnight's book, *Jesus Creed: Loving God, Loving Others* (Paraclete Press, 2004).

This all leads me to this observation: When we talk about spiritual formation, what do we have in mind? Do we have in mind "spirituality" in some nebulous (individually shaped) sense, or do we know what a spiritually formed person looks like? I am suggesting the Bible, and really the entire Christian tradition, [provides] two or three major images: first, the **Shema-Jesus Creed tradition,** where a spiritually formed person loves God and loves others; second, the rather significant category so often stated where we strive for humans who become shaped by the "image of Christ"; and the third one is this: people who are led by the Spirit of God.

I would take any of the three [I think they are all really saying the same thing], and I would suggest that we shape all of our discussion about spiritual formation around such outcomes, and stop measuring things that are easy to measure (church attendance, baptism, filled-out discipleship booklets, etc.) and start measuring, or striving for, what most matters—humans who have come into contact with God in such a way that they are led into union with God and communion with others, for the good of others and the world.

• Shane Wood: **Spiritual formation happens in an authentic community**

I approach this comment with great respect, understanding who I am and who I am engaging with in conversation.

Being from the "postmodern generation," I am encouraged with the possibilities of spiritual formation described by Mr. McLaren. I think we have measured the maturity of a Christian far too long off of the attendance sheets to various programs and functions (or participation with the institution). The maturity/spirituality of a person is much deeper than mere presence at an event; it is about the infiltration of the spirit by the Spirit. This seems to be the motivation of Mr. McLaren in his seven-fold approach to spiritual formation. I would contest, however, that a postmodern would not and is not looking for the seven elements to enrich their lives, but rather they are looking for the key to receiving knowledge, experience, relationships, practices, suffering, service, and time: namely, community. What the postmodern thinker and the postmodern generation are pushing for is a deeper connection with an authentic community.

Postmoderns have grown up in a world entrenched with disappointment. With the failure of modernity (promising exhaustive solutions through scientific methods that have led to an increase in deaths, wars, and catastrophes), the assault from society (forced agendas, overt immorality, and biased [opinions]), and the insecurity of true family (due to broken homes, wayward fathers, and abusive environments), postmoderns are left looking for a community in which they belong and can find identity. While there are some cautions to be [heeded], the postmodern generation seems to be shifting [from] a loss of identity to a trusted community.

This is a perfect playing ground for a Holy Spirit that has existed in a **perichoretic** community throughout eternity. To a postmodern, knowledge, experience, relationships (a given), practices, suffering, service, and time only have practical meaning within a community. (This is not to say that truth only exists within a community or is culturally/historically conditioned, which I personally reject, but that truth has practical meaning only in a context of community.) In other words, experiences without a community mean nothing, but experiences within a community mean everything. Service without community means nothing, but service within community means everything. Suffering without community means nothing, but suffering within community means everything. The reason why

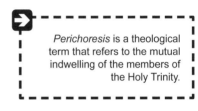

Perichoresis is a theological term that refers to the mutual indwelling of the members of the Holy Trinity.

this way of thinking seems so foreign to many people is because we are so accustomed to our individualism; reverting back to a theology based on community is incomprehensible.

The possible outcomes within Christianity could result in a reemergence of a neglected aspect of God: namely, transcendence (most evident in the Old Testament communal worship context). While the immanent Savior is still a key part in a postmodern's life, the reason for the importance is tied up in community. For without the Savior, the community would not be possible (body of Christ). Postmoderns are more enamored with the pictures of Revelation 21 and 22, a community with the Trinity who has suffered the same kind of painful experiences they have in their personal lives. We should grab ahold of the fact that a postmodern is able to identify keenly with a group led by a slain lamb, because that is exactly what we are.

The seven-fold approach to spiritual formation can only exist in an authentic community of suffering servants, in which the Spirit engages the individuals of the community and sanctifies them (or spiritually transforms them) for the sake of the eschatological community. We were created for community: community with God, community with creation, and community with each other (Genesis 1–3 stands as the loss of that three-fold community and Revelation 21–22 stands as the reinstitution of that three-fold community). In short, postmodernity looks to recapture what was destroyed by modernity: namely, an authentic community.

- Myron Bradley Penner: **Changing spiritual formation agendas**

I am very grateful for Brian's contribution both to this conversation and to the wider dialogue emerging on how we are to be faithful followers of Jesus Christ in the shift from modernity to postmodernity. I find his blog on spiritual formation to be critical for the latter task. I profoundly resonate with his description of modern evangelical spiritual growth paradigms and methods. Indeed, as with most other things, there has been an almost mechanical understanding of how God will work in our lives and how we will grow up in him: "If we just do the appropriate actions, results will follow." I think what Brian offers us here goes a long way toward a spirituality that can sustain us in these postmodern times.

I find what facilitates the sort of discussion through which Brian is guiding us is a complete shift in the agenda for spiritual growth. The more mechanically we conceive of spiritual growth, the more: 1) the onus is on us to achieve spiritual growth for ourselves, that is 2) quantifiably measurable by certain standards that inevitably become burdensome and guilt-producing. In other words, our model and practice of spiritual growth becomes a form of legalism and bondage, rather than joyous participation with God in his kingdom, as we move "higher up and further in," as C. S. Lewis might say. The two ideas that stand out to me are that spiritual growth—or just Christian spirituality in general—is more about the process than it is about achieving "measurable outcomes" and, correspondingly, spiritual growth is not our responsibility to achieve. The psalmist writes that "Unless the LORD builds the house, its builders labor in vain" (Psalm 127:1). Our responsibility in spiritual growth is to seek God and his kingdom above everything else, and to learn what it means to dwell in Christ in the very way he dwells with his Father in the blessed communion of the Holy Spirit. The very practical things Brian has to say help us achieve that end.

- Paula Spurr: **The magic number**

Oh how quickly we grab the list. Brian has given us seven things to do!! Quick, let's make pamphlets!! Sorry, I *am* chuckling as I write this, and humor often doesn't translate into written responses.

I don't think the point is that now we have an exhaustive list for our spiritual formation, but that we have to put away the old lists and expand our thinking, let go of the control of our spiritual formation, and put it solidly back into the hands of God. I appreciate the expanded look at what contributes to spiritual formation, but I'm not going to look at it like a recipe. It's not a scientific formula. $E = MC^2$ doesn't even hold in all situations, just ask a ray (or is it a particle?) of light trying to escape a black hole.

- Christy: **Spiritual nurturing, not forming**

I think that asking what spiritual formation looks like in a postmodern context, or what our outcomes should be, is the wrong question. There is an assumption behind [these questions] that I disagree with—that someone somewhere can decide what that should look like for everybody. If you start with a top-down model—where we come up with some abstract ideal which we then try to get everybody to live up to—then you come up with systems that don't make sense to a whole lot of people. I spent a decade working with low-income urban youth, and I can assure you that their process of spiritual formation needs to be very different from the youth who were popping pain pills every five minutes. For them—as for most of the world—suffering is the core experience out of which their spiritual formation grows.

Rather than asking, "How is everybody supposed to do this?" I think we should be asking people, "Where are you now? How is God present or not present in this? Where do you think you might be headed?" If we really believe that the Spirit is in us, then perhaps spiritual formation is a matter of calling out and nurturing what is already there (*especially* for children and youth), rather than trying to impose correct spirituality on a blank slate. I'm more interested in helping young people develop a spiritual center than I am in getting them to live up to an abstract ideal.

- James Walton: **Top-down models don't work**

Christy: I believe this is part of the realization that has been occurring as part of [emerging churches], which from my understanding was born out of many of these postmodern concerns. We've come to recognize that having a top-down model doesn't work all the time. There are so many different people, who have within them different gifts, and those gifts can be repressed if everyone is being conformed to a singular model.

I don't believe that what has been proposed with [Brian's] seven elements is a new structure for getting to that top-down goal. Rather, with more than just one or two facets of spiritual formation there is flexibility in the process and many different outcomes. In this context, spiritual transformation can result in the maturation of a Christian community—which is made up of artists, teachers, counselors, musicians, bakers/chefs, coaches, and whatever else you could imagine. The people and the Spirit can work together to transform themselves and their community to meet the needs of the world around them.

I think an excellent illustration, and a very biblical one, would be that of seeds. Let's say you came upon a bag full of a mixture of plant seeds. Scooping out a small handful, you decide to plant ten seeds, one each in a small paper cup. You place the ten cups in the kitchen window, which you know gets plenty of sun, and water them daily. At first, all the seeds start to sprout, but just as quickly most of them start to wither and struggle. You see, some of those plants love the sunlight but only require a little water. Others like the shade and plenty of water, and perhaps some just don't like being inside. If we can differentiate the care we give to these seedlings, we can nurture them into the beautiful plants they are meant to be. In contrast, if we stick to one form of care, some will die, some will flourish, and others will limp along in a state of mediocre health. We need to remember that each seed is different, and no matter how much we hope they all turn out to be [good seed], it is not within our power to determine.

- Eric Mason: **The key to spiritual formation: obedience**

I am leading an emerging church in my town and many of the attenders are, shall we say, in need of formation. But for each the challenge they are called to overcome is quite different. Some have substance abuse problems, others are struggling with the loneliness that comes from divorce and adultery, still others are foster kids who have bounced from home to home. But I believe in each of their lives that there is a common denominator. God is requiring them to hear and obey. In my previous post I mentioned the [formerly demonized] Gerasene and his success as a disciple of Christ. He was told to go and tell and *not* to sit and learn at the feet of Jesus. Though that was the imperative for the Twelve, the Gerasene was the best disciple that he could be and fully formed in his discipleship in his moments of obedience. The Twelve were bad disciples when they disobeyed Jesus but good disciples when they obeyed him.

Thus, I think postmodern spiritual formation becomes a subjective experience that alters and shifts for each individual as we ask the question, "What is God asking me to do?" Then in our obedience we become formed in the image of Jesus. Therefore the only objective standard that we can apply to spiritual formation is the one that comes from God. Our spiritual formation ebbs and flows through the biorhythm of life and a journey in Christ and with the Scriptures.

If you will, the key to discipleship and spiritual formation is obedience, the most subjective and relative of personal propositions. Our job as leaders, then, becomes helping individuals and communities hear God clearly and then obey.

- James Walton: **Missional focus**

Eric: I wouldn't replace character transformation and spiritual aptitude with obedience as the primary goal of spiritual formation. The statement made by Brian is actually that these facets are "a primary goal," not *the* goal. I think we should keep our goal aligned with our mission, which I think is articulated well by this statement: "To be and make disciples of Jesus Christ in authentic community for the good of the world" (Brian McLaren, *A Generous Orthodoxy* [Grand Rapids: Zondervan, 2004], 107). Spiritual formation is a lifelong journey, and obedience certainly is important. However, obedience can be observed to be somewhat of

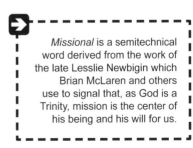

Missional is a semitechnical word derived from the work of the late Lesslie Newbigin which Brian McLaren and others use to signal that, as God is a Trinity, mission is the center of his being and his will for us.

an undercurrent to everything we encounter in our maturation as a disciple. In that frame of reference, I would say that obedience is an important aspect of spiritual formation, not the goal or key.

- Ellen Haroutunian: **Spiritual formation and room for mystery**

Of course the disciplines of spiritual formation are not a panacea, nor are they for everyone. However, as ancient as they are, they seem to offer a mysteriously good fit for many in the postmodern paradigm. Is there really ever anything new under the sun?

Before coming under spiritual direction, I had spent years in systematic Bible studies and the old exercise called "quiet time," which was meant to be a daily personal Bible study designed to help you find and follow application points for your life. Not that there's anything wrong with that! However, I have been concerned about how that approach to "knowing" God has encouraged a head-heart split in people. For example, I have a friend who has an amazing handle on the "absolutes" of his faith but has absolutely no idea how to love his spouse. He believes he knows what faith should produce in her personal thinking and feelings, but her tears have him confounded. What is important in the bottom-line realities of our lives? Perhaps people have learned that driving a stake into the ground of certainty may actually diminish our "knowing."

One cool thing which has come about through postmodernism is that people are more willing to sit for a while in questions, wonder, and mystery and not move too quickly toward demanding a definitive answer or a principle. The disciplines of spiritual formation do not start from a stance of attempted mastery over the Scriptures, but instead they are designed to facilitate a posture of receptivity which allows the Scriptures to speak to and shape us. The ancient practices of *lectio divina*, **examen**, gospel meditation, and others seem to round out what has been flattened by modern methodologies.

> *Lectio divina* is a Latin phrase that translates literally as "divine reading." It is also the name of a medieval (Benedictine) practice of reading Scripture for spiritual edification, which involves a slow, contemplative praying of the Scriptures.
>
> The *examen of conscience* is a five-step Jesuit prayer, prayed twice daily, that seeks to find the movement of the Holy Spirit in our daily lives.

The process they create offers an alternative way of "knowing" and seeking the presence of God.

Spiritual formation is not a rejection of the intellect, because it does involve an immersion in Scripture and attentiveness in meditation. However, it seems more holistic because my heart and my own story are also engaged. It seems that people are needing a sense of "home" and story within themselves, as well as [within their wider community]. To relate well to others, a person needs to be able to move out of a solid sense of self, which goes far deeper than the mind alone. Spiritual formation speaks into that center. More accurately, it helps us develop ears to hear God speak into that center and to shape within each unique person a real "me."

I agree with Brian's point about suffering. It is a given in this world. All the theology, philosophy, or political strategies we can know are unable to explain or alleviate this reality. Yet, centered hearts can create ways to lean into suffering alongside one another. One of the most meaningful symbols of the Christian narrative is the breaking of the bread, which symbolizes the body of Christ, broken for us. Throughout the New Testament, people who believe in Jesus are also called the body of Christ. There's a mysterious little passage in Luke (24:35) about a postresurrection appearance of Jesus. His friends who saw him reported later that he was "made known to them in the breaking of the bread" (NRSV). I can't help but wonder if the broken bread in these times is us, and as we lean into life and suffering with each other, perhaps Jesus will be made known.

• Brian McLaren: **Spiritual formation is missional formation!**

Thanks, all, for these very helpful responses. I wish I could have you as my editorial team whenever I write anything!

Based on your helpful input, here's what I'd do differently if I could start all over again.

1. I would have written a clearer disclaimer about the formulaic way of expressing things (with +'s and ='s). I wasn't trying to replace simplistic formulas with a more complex one, but instead I wanted to complexify the situation to such a degree that it pushed us beyond the formulaic. But I didn't make that clear enough,

and I appreciate those of you who were uncomfortable with the formulaic sound of my explanation.

2. It was pretty lame of me to leave out the Holy Spirit! "It goes without saying" is often the prelude to amnesia, so thanks for bringing this "minor" oversight up! As someone pointed out, it would be all too easy for my seven elements to become a longer and harder legalistic checklist if we forget that "we live and move and have our being" in God, and that God is at work in us "to will and do his good pleasure."

3. Scot McKnight's comment below was especially important, I think:

> When we talk about spiritual formation, what do we have in mind? Do we have in mind "spirituality" in some nebulous (individually shaped) sense, or do we know what a spiritually formed person looks like? I am suggesting the Bible, and really the entire Christian tradition [provides] two or three major images: first, the Shema-Jesus Creed tradition, where a spiritually formed person loves God and loves others; second, the rather significant category so often stated where we strive for humans who become shaped by the "image of Christ"; and the third one is this: people who are led by the Spirit of God.

> I would take any of the three [I think they are really saying the same thing], and I would suggest that we shape all of our discussion about spiritual formation around such outcomes, and stop measuring things that are easy to measure (church attendance, baptism, filled-out discipleship booklets, etc.) and start measuring, or striving for, what most matters—humans who have come into contact with God in such a way that they are led into union with God and communion with others, for the good of others and the world.

> That question of outcomes—"What is spiritual formation *for*?"—is so important, and I appreciate Scot's clarifications, and I agree wholeheartedly.

4. I just finished reading Kenzo's posting on "Evangelical and Post/ Modern Others" (What a treasure!), and it makes me want to take that question of outcomes one step further. If the making of (or spiritual formation of) disciples is what we're doing, we need to remember that disciples are trained *for* something. And putting disciple-making in the context of Jesus' life and message, I think we need to talk about spiritual formation *for* participation in the kingdom of God. In other words (as someone wisely said already), spiritual formation is also missional formation. We are being formed to love God and neighbors, to participate in the mission of the kingdom of God, which involves God's will being done on earth as it is in heaven. We could form people into practitioners of a privatized, internal, mystical, "satisfying" faith that helped keep them oblivious to the injustices, say, of colonialism. Or we could form people into agents in the kingdom of God, which always involves seeking God's justice in the world. In other words, I'm wondering if by talking about spiritual formation outside the context of mission and justice in my original posting, I've unintentionally perpetuated exactly the kind of Western Christianity that produced people who prayed, read the Bible, felt close to God—and held slaves, stole lands from North American indigenous peoples, mistreated women, exploited God's creation, etc., etc.

All of this makes me see why conversation like this is so important. I know I'm learning a lot from this.

NOTES

BLOG 1, THREAD 1

1. See Francis Schaeffer, *He Is There and He Is Not Silent* (Wheaton: Tyndale, 1972).

2. See Jacques Derrida, *Limited Inc*, ed. Gerald Graff, trans. Samuel Weber and Jeffrey Mehlman (Evanston, IL: Northwestern University Press, 1988).

3. See Jacques Derrida, *Acts of Religion*, trans. Gil Anidjar (London: Routledge, 2001).

BLOG 1, THREAD 2

1. See Richard Rorty, *Objectivity, Relativism, and Truth* (Cambridge: Cambridge University Press, 1991).

2. See Richard Rorty, *Philosophy and Social Hope* (London: Penguin, 1999).

3. Previously cited.

BLOG 1, THREAD 4

1. See René Descartes, *Meditations on First Philosophy: In Which the Existence of God and the Distinction of the Soul from the Body Are Demonstrated*, 3rd ed., trans. Donald A. Cress (Indianapolis: Hackett, 1993)

2. Descartes, *Meditations*, 13.

BLOG 2

1. Alister McGrath makes this observation in *A Passion for Truth: The Intellectual Coherence of Evangelicalism* (Downers Grove, IL: InterVarsity, 1996), 23.

2. A classic North American evangelical statement of the gospel as the "formal principle" of evangelicalism is found in Kenneth S. Kantzer, "Unity and Diversity in Evangelical Faith," in *The Evangelicals: What They Believe, Who They Are, Where They Are Changing*, rev. ed, eds. David F. Wells and John D. Woodbridge (Grand Rapids: Baker, 1975), 58–87. The literature

is immense and growing, but for more on what I am calling historical-theological treatments of evangelicalism, some which emphasize more the historical than the theological, others which emphasize the theological over the historical, see Mark A. Noll, *American Evangelicalism: An Introduction* (Oxford: Blackwell, 2001); George Marsden, *Fundamentalism and American Culture: The Shaping of Evangelicalism 1870–1925* (Oxford: Oxford University Press, 1980); David Bebbington, *Evangelicalism in Britain: A History from the 1730's to the 1980's* (London: Unwin Hyman, 1989); Stanley J. Grenz, *Renewing the Center: Evangelical Theology in a Post-Theological Era* (Grand Rapids: Baker, 2000), esp. chap. 2 and 3; Alister E. McGrath, *Evangelicals and the Future of Christianity* (Downers Grove, IL: InterVarsity, 1995); and John G. Stackhouse Jr., "Evangelical Theology Should Be Evangelical," in *Evangelical Futures*, ed. John Stackhouse (Grand Rapids: Baker, 2000), 39–58.

3. Any model one adopts is reductionist and inadequate at some level. The model I suggest sees evangelicalism as existing in a tension between two essential poles, as this idea of a bipolar phenomenon leaves plenty of room for diverse configurations and many more attributes between the poles. For a more thorough and historical treatment of evangelicalism's defining characteristics, see especially David Bebbington, *Evangelicalism in Britain*, 2–17, in which he draws the classic evangelical quadrangle of conversionism ("new birth"), biblicism (biblical authority), activism (evangelism), and crucicentrism (soteriological centrality of the cross).

4. The theological emphases are broader than just Scripture and preeminently include the divine-human nature of Jesus Christ and the substitutionary and sacrificial nature of Christ's death on the cross.

5. Inerrancy, however, appears to be a predominantly North American emphasis. In Britain, for example, it is enough to be an evangelical (in regard to Scripture) if one affirms Scripture as the final authority for Christian belief and practice, however that authority is conceived.

6   Carl F. H. Henry, *God, Revelation and Authority*, vol. 3 (Waco: Word, 1979), 477.

BLOG 2, THREAD 3

1. See Charles Hodge, *Systematic Theology*, 3 volumes (Grand Rapids: Eerdmans, 1986).

BLOG 3, THREAD 1

1. See Robert Audi, *Epistemology: A Contemporary Introduction to the Theory of Knowledge*, 2nd ed. (London: Routledge, 1998).

2. Editors' note: See especially Steven Best and Douglas Kellner, *Postmodern Theory: Critical Interrogations* (New York: Guilford Press, 1991).

BLOG 4

1. By "traditional evangelical" I refer to the dominant evangelical consensus in North America in the twentieth century, whose dominant focus has been on the doctrine of Scripture and included inerrancy as the linchpin of that doctrine.

2. Søren Kierkegaard, *Søren Kierkegaard's Journals and Papers*, vol. 1, trans. and ed. Howard V. Hong and Edna H. Hong (Bloomington, IN: Indiana University Press, 1967), 84.

3. I have benefited much from John Franke's emphasis on this aspect of Barth's thought. See John R. Franke, "The Nature of Theology: Culture, Language, and Truth," in *Christianity and the Postmodern Turn: Six Views*, ed. Myron B. Penner (Grand Rapids: Brazos, 2005), 209–10.

4. Vanhoozer first used the term "postpropositionalism" in "The Voice and the Actor: A Dramatic Proposal about the Ministry and Minstrels of Theology," in *Evangelical Futures: A Conversation on Theological Method*, ed. John G. Stackhouse Jr. (Grand Rapids: Baker, 2000), 75ff. Vanhoozer has since developed and nuanced his use of the term in Vanhoozer, *The Drama of Doctrine: A Canonical-Linguistic Approach to Christian Theology* (Louisville: Westminster John Knox, 2005). In order to protect the innocent, I want to emphasize that, while I have borrowed the terminology and basic concept of "postpropositionalism" from Vanhoozer, mine is not necessarily his meaning of the term.

5. Kevin J. Vanhoozer, "Lost in Interpretation? Truth, Scripture and Hermeneutics," *Journal of the Evangelical Theological Society* (March 2005): 97ff.

6. This concept of "triangulation" screams out for clarification, which I simply do not have room to provide. Perhaps we can speak more of this in the ensuing dialogue.

BLOG 5

1. D. A. Carson, *The Gagging of God: Christianity Confronts Pluralism* (Grand Rapids: Zondervan, 1996), 10.

2. Charles Jencks, "The Post-Modern Agenda," in *The Post-Modern Reader*, ed. Charles Jencks (New York: Saint Martin, 1992), 10–39.

3. David Harvey, *The Condition of Postmodernity: An Inquiry into the Origins of Cultural Change* (Oxford: Blackwell, 1990), 9.

4. Robert Young, *Postcolonialism: An Historical Introduction* (Oxford: Blackwell, 2001), 136.

5. Carson, *The Gagging of God*, 10.

6. Catherine Keller, Michael Nausner, and Mayra Rivera, eds., *Postcolonial Theologies: Divinity and Empire* (Saint Louis: Chalice Press, 2004), 11.

7. Linda Hutcheon, *A Poetics of Postmodernism: History, Theory, Fiction* (New York: Routledge, 1988).

8. Jean-François Lyotard, *The Postmodern Condition: A Report on Knowledge*, trans. Geoff Bennington and Brian Massumi (Minneapolis: University of Minnesota Press, 1984), xxiii.

9. Ibid.

10. Mudimbe uses the expression "colonial library" to identify the body of literature that grew around the modern project of colonization. Cf. Valentin Y. Mudimbe, *The Invention of Africa: Gnosis, Philosophy, and the Order of Knowledge* (Bloomington, IN: Indiana University Press, 1988).

11. Ania Loomba, *Colonialism/Postcolonialism* (New York: Routledge, 1998), 43–44.

12. See Mudimbe, *The Invention of Africa*, and Edward W. Said, *Orientalism* (New York: Vintage Books, 1994).

13. Robert J. C. Young, *White Mythologies: Writing History and the West* (London: Routledge, 1990), 19.

14. Tite Tiénou, "The Right to Difference: The Common Roots of African Theology and African Philosophy," *African Journal of Evangelical Theology* 9 (1990): 24–34.

15. Steven Connor, *Postmodernist Culture: An Introduction to Theories of the Contemporary* (Oxford: Blackwell, 1989), 232.

BLOG 6

1. Here I am following Merold Westphal very closely in both the form and content of my suggestion. See his wonderful essay, "Prolegomena to Any Future Philosophy of Religion That Will Be Able to Come Forth as Prophecy," in *Kierkegaard's Critique of Reason and Society* (Macon, GA: Mercer University Press, 1982),1–18.

2. Westphal, "Prolegomena to Any Future Philosophy of Religion," 10.

3. Once again, the phrase is Westphal's. See Merold Westphal, "Kierkegaard and the Logic of Insanity," in *Kierkegaard's Critique*, 85–104.

4. Quoted in Westphal, *Kierkegaard's Critique*, 87.

5. Stanley Hauerwas, *With the Grain of the Universe: The Church's Witness and Natural Theology* (Grand Rapids: Brazos Press, 2001), 207.

6. Merold Westphal makes the distinction between meganarratives and metanarratives in *Overcoming Onto-Theology: Toward a Postmodern Christian Faith* (New York: Fordham University Press, 2001), xiii.

7. Søren Kierkegaard, *Works of Love* (Princeton, NJ: Princeton University Press), 335 (italics added).

BLOG 6, THREAD 2

1. Søren Kierkegaard, *Concluding Unscientific Postscript to Philosophical Fragments*, vol. 1 (Princeton, NJ: Princeton University Press, 1992); the following quotations are from page 201.

BLOG 7

1. *The Lord of the Rings: The Fellowship of the Ring*, directed by Peter Jackson, New Line Cinema Productions, 2002.

2. See Ron Sider, *The Scandal of the Evangelical Conscience* (Grand Rapids: Baker, 2005).

3. Daniel Johnson, "Contrary Hopes: Evangelical Christianity and the Decline Narrative," in *The Future of Hope: Christian Tradition amid Modernity and Postmodernity*, ed. Miroslav Volf and William Katerberg (Grand Rapids: Eerdmans, 2004), 33.

4. Miroslav Volf, *Exclusion and Embrace: A Theological Exploration of Identity, Otherness and Reconciliation* (Nashville: Abingdon, 1996), 74.

5. C. S. Lewis, *The Horse and His Boy* (New York: Collier Books, 1970), 192–93.

6. John Milbank, "The Gospel of Affinity," in *The Future of Hope: Christian Tradition amid Modernity and Postmodernity*, 159.

7. Miroslav Volf, *After Our Likeness: The Church as the Image of the Trinity* (Grand Rapids: Eerdmans, 1998), 7.

8. Zygmunt Bauman, quoted in Dave Tomlinson, *The Post-Evangelical* (Grand Rapids: Zondervan, 2003), 84.

9. *Eternal Sunshine of the Spotless Mind*, directed by Charlie Kaufman, Focus Features, 2004.

10. *Garden State*, directed by Zach Braff, Miramax Films, 2004.

11. Craig Detweiler and Barry Taylor, *A Matrix of Meanings: Finding God in Pop Culture* (Grand Rapids: Baker, 2003), 52.

A NEW KIND OF CONVERSATION

In the midst of the cultural and intellectual upheavals of postmodernity in Western society, evangelicalism finds itself in the middle of a conversation about its own identity and future.

Whereas postmodernism is typically discussed in a traditional book form—an edited volume with essays—the format of this book seeks to place the discussion in a form that is consistent with its content. Using the motif of the blog, *A New Kind of Conversation* is an experimental book that enters into this conversation with five evangelical leaders and academics acting as the primary bloggers: Brian McLaren, Bruce Ellis Benson, Ellen Haroutunian, Mabiala Kenzon, and Myron Bradley Penner.

Originally posted on anewkindofconversation.com, people all over the world were invited to blog on topics relevant to the issue of postmodernism and evangelicalism such as:

- What is "Postmodernism"?
- Evangelical Faith and (Postmodern) Others
- Postmodernism and Spiritual Formation
- What is a Postmodern Evangelical?

This book, a distillation of that exchange, invites you to engage in this challenging and complex discussion. Welcome to the conversation!

MYRON BRADLEY PENNER is professor of Philosophy and Theology at Prairie College and lives in Three Hills, AB, Canada, with his wife and three daughters. Myron has a BS and MA from Liberty University, Virginia, and a PhD from New College, Edinburgh University. He is the co-chair of the Study Group for Evangelical Theology and Postmodernism at the Evangelical Theological Society and is the editor of (and contributor to) *Christianity and the Postmodern Turn: Six Views*.

HUNTER BARNES has a diverse background including professional work as an actor and writer. He has a deep interest in narrative theory and orality and scripture, and has been working on a project in the performance of scripture through the Gospel of Mark for the past three years. Hunter received his MA in Communication/Theatre Arts from Regent University in Virginia. Hunter lives in Zarephath, New Jersey with his wife and three daughters, and is the creative arts director for Zarephath Christian Church.

Theology / General

ISBN 978-1-932805-58-1

9 781932 805581

Paternoster:
thinking faith

www.authenticbooks.com/paternoster